Our Gratitude To

Josh & Dottie McDowell for taking us under their wings, believing in the project, and standing with us.

We are also deeply grateful to the two following people and the organizations they represent for sharing with us dozens of scholarly, sensitive and scriptural articles for the Appendices in this book:

Marilyn Adamson, leader within Cru and the founder and director of Everystudent.com.

S. Michael Houdmann, Founder, President, and CEO of Got Questions Ministries.

We are grateful to Need Him Global for agreeing to allow us to refer people to their ministry, thereby offering people a safe place to ask questions about Jesus and be able to talk to someone live.

We are grateful to Sonia Armour and Joel Craig for their invaluable insight in the beginning stages in the manuscript of this book and to Jeanne Cadeau for her superb proofreading.

LIGHT IN ACTION THANKS

The hundreds of volunteers who have acted, assisted, and translated,

Along with our beloved families & our churches,

Together with countless others, spread across the planet, who have courageously

Stood with us, mentored us, and gone to battle on their knees

So that *Tetelestai* could become a reality.

TETELESTAI

STUDY GUIDE

Copyright © 2018 by Light in Action INC

All rights reserved. No part of this publication may be reproduced, stored in a retrieval system, or transmitted in any form or by any means - electronic, mechanical, photocopying, recording, or otherwise - without the prior written permission of the publisher and copyright owners, except in the case of brief quotations embodied in critical articles or reviews.

All Scripture quotations unless otherwise noted are from the Holy Bible, New International Version®, NIV®, Copyright © 1973, 1978, 1984, 2011 by Biblica Inc ® Used by permission. All right reserved worldwide.

Scripture quotations in Got Questions Ministries articles, unless otherwise noted, are taken from: The Holy Bible, English Standard Version. ESV® Text Edition: 2016. Copyright © 2001 by Crossway Bibles, a publishing ministry of Good News Publishers.

Scripture texts in this work are taken from the *New American Bible, revised edition* © 2010, 1991, 1986, 1970 Confraternity of Christian Doctrine, Washington, D.C. and are used by permission of the copyright owner. All Rights Reserved. No part of the New American Bible may be reproduced in any form without permission in writing from the copyright owner.

Scripture texts in this work are taken from the *Holy Bible*, New Living Translation, copyright © 1996, 2004, 2015 by Tyndale House Foundation. Used by permission of Tyndale House Publishers, Inc., Carol Stream, Illinois 60188. All rights reserved.

Scripture texts in this work are taken from the New American Standard Bible (NASB) Copyright © 1960, 1962, 1963, 1968, 1971, 1972, 1973, 1975, 1977, 1995 by The Lockman Foundation

All Appendix articles from Got Questions Ministries, Copyright © 2002-2018, are used by permission. Got Questions Ministries has all rights reserved to their articles.

All Appendix articles from EveryStudent.com, Copyright © 2018, are used by permission. EveryStudent.com has all rights reserved to their articles.

Produced by: Light in Action INC.
1104 El Sonoro Dr.
Sierra Vista, Az, 85635

Cover & Interior Design: Light in Action INC.

ISBN-13: 978-1718645523
ISBN-10: 171864552X

STUDY GUIDE

ARLEN & CYNTHIA ISAAK

www.lightinaction.org

To Him who loved us

and has freed us from our sins by His blood...

TO HIM BE GLORY...FOREVER

Revelation 1:5,6

CONTENTS

CHAPTERS:

1 - In the Beginning……………………………………………………..11

2 - The Promise………………………………………………………….19

3 - Provision…………………………………………………………......25

4 - Deliverance………………………………………………...………..33

5 - The Law……………………………………………………………...41

6 - Atonement…………………………………………………………..49

7 - Lamb of God………………………………………………………...59

8 - Messiah……………………………………………………………...67

9 - Salvation……………………………………………………………..75

10 - It is Finished……………………………………………………..…83

11 - Eternal Life…………………………………………………………93

12 - What do You Believe?………………………………………..…103

APPENDIX:

Study Guide Appendix……………………………………………….115

Dates You Will Be Meeting

Fill out the dates you will be meeting to study each chapter.

CHAPTER	DATE & TIME
1 - In the Beginning	
2 - The Promise	
3 - Provision	
4 - Deliverance	
5 - The Law	
6 - Atonement	
7 - Lamb of God	
8 - Messiah	
9 - Salvation	
10 - It is Finished	
11 - Eternal Life	
12 - What do You Believe?	

BEFORE YOU BEGIN

Thirty Seconds:

Have you ever caught only 30 seconds of an action movie right in the thick of the most dramatic scene? Although the music is intense and the action is fast-paced, you don't know who all the characters are and you're unaware of the intricate plot. While those around you may be moved to tears when the hero gives his life to save someone, you find yourself disconnected and confused.

How could things have been different? Well, watching the movie from the beginning would have helped, wouldn't you say? For many people, their exposure to the Bible is similar to this example. If you could compare the Bible to a movie, then they've watched thirty seconds of most famous scenes…. but without understanding the plot.

Tetelestai:

In the most famous passage of the Bible, the Hero dies. Moments before He breathes His last breath, however, He proclaims a word: "Tetelestai." The word "*Tetelestai*" (Teh-TELL-eh-sty) is Greek for "It is Finished."
What exactly had Jesus finished…?
Why does this phrase have the potential to change human destiny?

In order to find these answers, we're going to start the Story of the Bible from the beginning, study several key narratives and unfold the plot. As we do, I hope the message of the Bible comes to life for you. It reveals the Story of a God who passionately loves humanity and will pay the ultimate price for their rescue.

What does this have to do with you?

Seeking Answers?

If you are spiritually curious, we want to walk this journey with you. We want you to feel comfortable as you ask questions, investigate, and wrestle with what the Bible has to say. We pray this Study will put the pieces of the Bible together in a way that will allow you to catch a breathtaking glimpse of God's love, and how much He desires to have a relationship with you.

Going Deeper?

If you already have a relationship with God, we pray that throughout this Bible Study two things will happen:

First, we pray the beautiful truths of God's Word will soak into every part of your soul. Our desire is that you fall more deeply in love with God as you take a fresh look at the depths of what He has done for you.

Second, we pray that today you will already begin to think about with *whom* you are going to share His life. Perhaps a neighbor, a relative, a classmate or co-worker? As you grapple and engage with His Word, please see this as a valuable training time that will equip you to effectively share God's Eternal Story of Redemption with those who have never heard.

Walking through this together:

If you're doing the *Tetelestai* Bible Study in a group setting, please reach out to your facilitator. He or she has been equipped with supplementary materials that will help answer various questions you may have.

Regardless of whether you are doing this study on your own or in a group, we want to assist you along the way. In order to do that better, we've partnered with some incredible people who make answering questions about God their top priority! Don't hesitate to reach out with a question, comment or concern about your faith.

Chat with Someone or Ask Questions:

Talk to Someone Live	**Call:** 888-NeedHim (888-633-3446) **Chat Online:** www.chataboutJesus.com
Ask a Question	www.gotquestions.org
Ask a Question	www.everystudent.com
Contact Light in Action	Light in Action 1104 El Sonoro Dr. Sierra Vista, AZ, 85635 **Email:** tetelestai@lightinaction.org

CHAPTER 1

IN THE BEGINNING

With archaeological discoveries and astounding fulfillment of prophecies, the Bible is not only a trustworthy historical account but the Book that reveals the God you were created to know.

Only the Eternal God can Truly Satisfy Us:

There is a longing within every human heart. A hunger in the soul. A thirst that can't be satisfied. Deep inside, we long for something more, more than what is in our world. These longings cannot be satisfied by pursuing knowledge, pleasure, wealth and possessions. They are amplified as we search for meaning and purpose during the few days of our lives. There is only One who can bring meaning, fulfillment, joy and peace to your life. He is the only One who can fill the void and quench the thirst within our souls.

Until we find Him there is a restless yearning, a longing that He put in our hearts. Just as thirst is necessary to draw someone to water, these longings within our heart were meant to call us to God. Within the heart of every human being, He has placed eternity. Because of this, nothing but the Eternal God can truly satisfy us.

You can Know God Through the Bible:

It is through the Bible that you will be introduced to the Eternal God. The Bible is a collection of 66 individual writings called books. Even the name "Bible" comes from a Greek word that means "books" The Bible has been divided into two sections called the Old and New Testaments. To make reading easier, each book was divided up into chapters and verses. In the first few pages of your Bible you will usually find a list of these books. Follow along in your Bible to verify the accuracy of everything that you hear, so that your confidence will be in what God says!

God is the True Author of the Bible:

The Bible is the world's best seller! It is the most quoted, read and printed book in all of history. It has been translated into almost 2,500 languages. It has influenced and transformed lives throughout the ages. The Bible was written through 40 different men, over a period of 1,600 years, across 3 continents, and in 3 languages. Even though these authors came from a wide range of professions and lived in various locations during different time periods, the diverse manuscripts came together perfectly. **2 Timothy 3:16** and **2 Peter 1:21** affirm that God told these men what they should write. Over 3,800 times in the Bible you will find phrases emphasizing that God is the Author of the Bible, phrases such as **Jeremiah 1:2**, *"And the word of the LORD came to him…"*.

The Bible is Historically Accurate:

Throughout the ages, archeology has confirmed the accuracy of the Bible. Even the most minute details of little-known passages have proven to be historically sound. Take **Isaiah 20:1** for example. Historians questioned the veracity of the events described in the passage. In 1843, however, in northern Iraq, archaeologist Paul Émile Botta unearthed the palace of King Sargon. Astonishingly, engraved on the palace walls was a description of the very same events being described in **Isaiah 20:1**! With the Bible's help, renowned archaeologist Dr. Nelson Glueck discovered more than a thousand ancient sites in the Transjordan area, and another 500 in the Negev. In his book, *Rivers in the Desert,* Dr. Nelson Glueck stated that there has never been an archaeological discovery that has contradicted the Bible! Dr. William Ramsay, a Scottish professor and archeologist, concluded that because of the Bible's historical accuracy, it had to be the very words of God Himself.

Prophecies Confirm the Bible's Divine Authorship:

The Bible contains hundreds of prophecies foretelling future events. In **Psalm 22,** King David described crucifixion 400 years before it was used as a form of capital punishment. (**Isaiah 44:28**) Isaiah mentioned King Cyrus by name 150 years before his reign. (**Isaiah 39:5-7**) Isaiah also foretold the fall of Jerusalem 100 years before it was taken over by the Babylonians. In **Daniel 11** there are 135 prophecies so precise that they describe major alliances, battles, marriages and even murder. This same book, Daniel, foretold the rise and fall of the Babylonian, Medo-Persian, Grecian and Roman empires.

The Bible Tells One Eternal Story:

The Bible has one running plot that connects all the details and events together. Throughout all the drama and descriptions, there is one theme that makes the whole Story make sense. It is this central plot that we are going to watch unfold as we study this Book. So what is the "Eternal story of the Bible"? What better place to start than the beginning!

God is Eternal:

In the very first verse of the Bible, **Genesis 1:1**, we see that before time began, God already existed. God never had a beginning, nor will He have an end. That's hard for our minds to grasp because we humans are confined by time. We can talk about the past as we remember days that have gone by, but we cannot go back in time. We can make plans for tomorrow as we dream about the future, but we cannot go ahead in time even one minute! God, however is not like that! God is *outside* of time. God is present in the past, the present, and the future, all at the same time! (**Psalm 90:2**) He never changes. He never gets tired. He never diminishes. God is eternal!

God is All-Present:

Not only is God not limited by time, God is not limited by space. We humans are completely limited by space. No matter how much we would like to be in more than one place at a time, we cannot. No matter how fast we travel, or how much our schedule demands of us, we can only be in one place at a time. God is not like we are! The Bible says that God is all-present, or in other words: God is everywhere at the same time. (**Psalm 139:4,7-10**)

God is Triune:

There is something else we discover about God in the first four words of the Bible. The book of Genesis was written in Hebrew. The word for "God" in Hebrew is Elohim. In Hebrew, when you see an "im" on the end of the word, that usually signifies it is plural. Why then does the word for God, "Elohim", have an "im" on the end of it? This plural ending on the name for God is the first indication that we have in the Bible that the One God reveals Himself in three Persons.

Dr. Arnold Fruchtenbaum wrote that the Hebrew Scriptures portray God to be One in three Persons. The New Testament sheds even more light on the subject, revealing Him to be Father, Son, and Holy Spirit. Each One being eternal, equal, and distinct.

The truth is that God is infinite. For us humans, who are finite, to fully comprehend God would be like expecting little ants to be able to learn how to read! Just as it would be impossible for them to grasp even the most basic concepts of our language, it would be impossible for *us* to fully comprehend an infinite God! God has told us many things about His nature in the Bible that we must believe even without fully understanding.

God is All-Powerful; the Creator and Sustainer:

In **Genesis 1:1** we see that God is the Designer and Creator of everything that exists. By the power of His word He created everything. (**Genesis 1:3**) God sustains the universe in all of its vastness. (**Hebrews 1:3**) What then could be impossible for God? More than 50 times in the Bible God is described as being all-powerful. When you face a serious problem or when your future seems to offer you no hope, with whom do you seek counsel? Where do you go for help? The all-powerful God of the Bible says to you: "Come to me! Trust in me. I care for you."

God is All-Knowing:

Have you ever considered how much knowledge it would take to design the heavens and the earth? Whether looking through a telescope at our vast galaxy or peering through a microscope at finely tuned biological organisms, we will never fully understand the complexities and intricacies of our universe. The Designer of the universe does, however! The Bible says that God is all-knowing. (**Psalm 147:5**)

Far more amazing is the fact that this incredible God chose to know you and me personally! So many times we feel so alone wondering, "Does anyone even care that I exist?" It is through this Book, the Bible, that you will be introduced to Someone who not only knows your name, but chooses to know every single thing about you. (**Psalm 139:1,2,4,13,16**)

You Were Created for this Relationship:

You were created by this Wonderful God. He is the One your heart longs for! This is why God has given us His Word: the Bible. Knowing Him is the reason for this life. He offers you a relationship that goes beyond this life and lasts forever. Today could be just ...*the Beginning.*

PERSONAL & RELEVANT

Topic One: Brevity of life & the search for fulfillment

Question: What events or instances have reminded you of how short or fragile life is?

Have you ever been shocked at how much someone has aged when you haven't seen them in awhile? What are some other examples you can think of?

_____

_____

Question: Because people innately know life is short, they are constantly searching for fulfillment and meaning in their life. From constantly switching phones to constantly switching boyfriends, what examples of the restless search for fulfillment can you think of? Do those things ever satisfy?

_____

_____

Topic Two: The Bible

Question: What was the evidence presented for the Bible being God's Word? Which two facts did you find the most compelling?

You can refresh your memory by glancing through some of the notes provided.

_____

_____

Topic Three: Relationship with God

Question: How do you get to know someone and how do these same principles apply to getting to know God? Whether it's on a social media page or in person, how someone expresses themselves shows what they care about and what they think. How do we know what God thinks and what He has to say?

_____

_____

WHAT DOES THIS MEAN FOR *YOU*?

1. Only God can truly satisfy:

"There is a longing within the heart of every human being. This week, take time out to notice the brevity of life and the restlessness that drives people everywhere to pursue the satisfaction of the thirst within their souls. Remember that these longings in your heart were meant to call you to God, the only One who can truly satisfy you."

2. The Bible was written for you:

"To record the words of the Bible, God used forty different authors, living in different time periods, in different places, writing in three different languages. Yet, amazingly from these diverse manuscripts, one eternal story emerges. You too, can examine the thousands of archaeological discoveries that verify the Bible's accuracy and the astounding prophecies foretelling future events. As you do, remember that the very words of this Book were written by God for you."

3. God cares for you:

"In Genesis 1:1, we saw how God is eternal and triune. We also saw how He is all-powerful, creating the world by simply speaking! The Challenges you face in your life may seem impossible, but they are not impossible for this Almighty God who says, "Come to Me! I care for you!"

4. God desires a relationship with you:

"We saw God is all-present and all-knowing. As the Designer of this universe, He understands its every single intricate detail and function. You may feel alone, thinking no one even knows you exist. But this same God chooses to know you personally and already knows everything about you. Now you have an opportunity to get to know Him through His Word, the Bible."

Read it for yourself:

Ecclesiastes 2	A snapshot of King Solomon's search for meaning.
Ecclesiastes 12:13,14	King Solomon's conclusion.
II Peter 1:20-21 & II Timothy 3:16	The authors of the Bible were told by God what to write.
Genesis 1	God created the world; He is eternal, triune, all-powerful, all-knowing and all-present.
Psalm 139:1-16	God not only knows everything about you but cares deeply for you.
Isaiah 55:1-11	God's invitation for all who are thirsty to come to Him for satisfaction.

Dig Deeper:

Why You Can Believe the Bible:	**Pg. 117**
Exciting archaeological discoveries:	**Pg. 129**

Memorize this:

"You have searched me, LORD, and you know me." **Psalm 139:1**

CHAPTER 2

THE PROMISE

A loving relationship with God is broken when Adam and Eve sin. God, however, promises to send a Deliverer who will pay the ultimate price to restore the broken relationship between God and mankind.

We were Created for a Relationship with God:

God wants you to know Him. In Genesis, the first book of the Bible, we read that this relationship was God's plan from the very beginning of time. Unlike the rest of His creation, the man and woman were created in the image of God. (**Genesis 1:26-27**) They would not merely be physical beings, for God created humans with a spiritual side capable of knowing and loving Him. God Himself walked and talked with Adam and Eve in the Garden of Eden.

God Gave Adam and Eve a Choice:

God did not force Adam and Eve to love and obey Him. He wanted them to choose to love Him; for real love is only love if it is a choice. God gave Adam and Eve this choice by commanding them not to eat the fruit from the Tree of the Knowledge of Good and Evil. (**Genesis 2:16-17**) God gave them a simple command with clear consequences: if they ate the fruit of that tree they would die. God is the author of life. To reject God, is to reject life. If you reject life, then you are choosing death.

Satan came to the Garden as a serpent:

(**Genesis 3:1**) While this passage in Genesis does not reveal the serpent's identity, several other passages in the Bible provide us with the answer. God created a multitude of spirit beings called angels. They were made to worship and serve God alone. **Isaiah 14:12** tell us of an important angel named Lucifer. At some point in time, this good angel became wicked (**Ezekiel 28:15,17**) Lucifer, consumed with pride, desired to usurp God's throne. (**Isaiah 14:14**) Because God is holy, completely pure with nothing evil in Him, He will not allow anyone evil to remain in His presence. Lucifer and the angels who joined him in this rebellion were expelled from Heaven. (**Ezekiel 28:16**)

From that point on, the Bible refers to Lucifer as Satan, and the rebellious angels are known today as demons or unclean spirits. The Bible tells us that one day they will be thrown into a horrible place called the Lake of Fire, to be punished for the rest of eternity. Today, Satan knows his time on earth is limited and seeks to destroy God's creation by enticing them to rebel against God.

Satan Tempted Adam and Eve:

In the Garden of Eden, Satan accused God of lying to Adam and Eve. Satan told them they would not die if they ate the fruit from the Tree of the Knowledge of Good and Evil. (**Genesis 3:1-4**) Satan wanted them to doubt God's *word*. (**Genesis 3:5**) By trying to convince Adam and Eve that God could not be trusted and was trying to keep something good away from them, Satan sought to cause Adam and Eve to doubt God's *love*. (**Genesis 3:6**) Adam and Eve listened to Satan's lies and chose to disobey God. **Romans 5:12** says that at that moment, sin entered the world. Sin is anything that goes against the perfect character of God.

Sin Broke their Relationship with God:

When Adam and Eve sinned they were filled with the feelings that sin brings: shame, guilt and fear. (**Genesis 3:7**) Trying to make coverings out of leaves was a desperate attempt to deal with these feelings, but the shame they felt went down to their very soul. Before sinning, they had walked and talked with God, but now they were running away from Him! (**Genesis 3:8**) Despite the fact that Adam and Eve had disobeyed God and rejected Him, God did not give up on them. Instead, God reached out to them. (**Genesis 3:9**)

Sin Affected the Entire Earth:

When God gave Adam and Eve a chance to confess their sin, (**Genesis 3:10-13**) neither Adam nor Eve admitted that what they had done was wrong. Regardless, they stood completely guilty before a holy God. Their sin would now have consequences that affected the entire earth. (**Genesis 3:14-19**) Their once-perfect world would now produce thorns and thistles. Their day-to-day life would be one of hard work and sweat. All animal life would suffer. Hardship, pain, tears and sorrow would now be a part of human existence. Harmony and peace would be disrupted by evil. All would suffer because of sin.

The Payment for Sin is Death:

Romans 6:23 states that the wages, or payment for sin is death. From that day forward, all people would age and die, returning to the same ground from which Adam had been made. (**Genesis 3:19**) After physical death, the Bible says each person will be judged by God. (**Hebrews 9:27**) If someone were to die with the condemnation of their sins upon them, they would be separated from God forever. Adam and Eve had chosen to obey Satan. Because of this, they were in danger of facing the same destiny as Satan: eternal death in the Lake of Fire.

The Promise of a coming Deliverer:

Instead of instantly sentencing Adam and Eve to eternal condemnation, however, God chose at that moment to give a stunning promise. (**Genesis 3:15**) God promised that one day a Son would be born who would not have a human father. This Son would one day crush Satan's head, but in the process, the Son himself would be hurt. In this promise to Adam and Eve, God not only foretold the destruction of their enemy, but the deliverance of humanity. This promised Son would liberate humanity from their slavery to sin and death. He would restore the broken relationship between God and man. This was the first promise of the coming Deliverer.

An Innocent One Died to Cover them:

Adam and Eve had tried desperately to deal with the shame they felt because of their sin. God Himself, in His love and mercy, covered Adam and Eve with animal skins. (**Genesis 3:21**) In order to make garments of skin an animal had to die! Think about it: That day in the Garden, who disobeyed God? Who deserved to die? Did that animal deserve to die? No! Adam and Eve were the ones who disobeyed God. Even though they deserved to die, God provided an innocent one to die in order to cover them.

Adam and Eve could not resolve the problem of their sin, only God could. Unlike the clothing made from leaves, these garments of skin were *God's* plan done in *God's* way. God covered their shame by clothing them in the one who had died for them. God was beginning to reveal more of His plan and the ultimate price that would be one day be paid in order to rescue humanity.

PERSONAL & RELEVANT

Topic One: Real love must be a choice

Question: How did God give Adam and Eve a choice in the Garden instead of programming them to automatically obey Him?

_____
_____

Question: What does that say about the type of relationship that God desires to have with humanity?

_____
_____

Topic Two: Tactics of the enemy

Question: We saw how Satan tempted Adam and Eve to doubt God's love and God's Word. How do we see Satan influencing people in those two areas today? How have you experienced this in your own life?

_____
_____

Topic Three: Clothing made from leaves

Question: Driven by shame, guilt and fear, Adam and Eve tried to make clothing out of leaves. What type of things do people do today in an attempt to make things right or to alleviate their consciences? *What versions of "leaf clothes" do you see in our culture?*

_____
_____

CHAPTER 2: THE PROMISE

WHAT DOES THIS MEAN FOR *YOU*?

1. God's plan is for a relationship with you.

"God's plan from the beginning of time was for a special relationship with humanity. God also desires a relationship with you! Like Adam and Eve, God made you in His image, with a spiritual side capable of knowing and loving Him. God wants you to trust Him and to believe in His Word."

2. Satan's tactics are the same with you.

"We often think that a message from Satan would be overtly evil. But when Satan came to talk to Adam and Eve he seemed harmless and simply started a conversation with them. Be aware that Satan will use the same tactics with you. Often he will use methods that appear harmless or even attractive. He will do whatever it takes to get you to doubt God's Word and to doubt God's love."

3. Only God can resolve the problem of your sin.

"When Adam and Eve disobeyed God, their relationship with Him was broken. In desperation, they tried to cover themselves with leaves. Just as Adam and Eve's leaf clothes were completely inadequate to take away the shame and guilt of their sin, your good works will never be enough. You cannot pay for your sins through your own efforts. Only God can resolve the problem of your sin."

4. God is calling you.

"Even though Adam and Eve had disobeyed God and run away from Him, because of His love, God Himself reached out to them. This is the same God who is searching after you. He loves you and is also calling your name. God promised Adam and Eve He would one day send a Deliverer who would rescue humanity. This was a promise for all people. It was a Promise for you."

Read it for yourself:

Genesis 1&2	God creates the world.
Ezekiel 38: 12-17	Satan rebels against God.
Genesis 3	Adam and Eve disobey God.
Genesis 1	God created the world; He is eternal, triune, all-powerful, all-knowing and all-present.
Romans 5:12	Adam's sin was passed down.
Romans 6:23	The payment for sin death.
Genesis 3:15	The promise of the Deliverer

Dig Deeper

Who is the Devil and is he a threat?	**Pg. 132**
Satan is our enemy	**1 Peter 5:8**
We love God because He first loved us.	**1 John 4:19**

Memorize this:

"For all have sinned and fall short of the glory of God." **Romans 3:23**

CHAPTER 3

PROVISION

In a judgment of floodwaters God provides One way of escape for all who believe. Years later, in a divine test with Abraham, a striking picture is painted of a future substitute who will give His life for the world

All People are Born Sinners:

Because of Adam and Eve's sin, all people in the world are born sinners, separated from God. (**Romans 5:12**) Yet God's desire was still for a relationship with all people. God provided a way that they could approach Him and be His friend. Each person, however, would have to *choose* for themselves, whether or not, they wanted a relationship with God.

The Majority of Humanity had Rejected God:

Genesis 4 and 5 give us details of a highly advanced civilization with agriculture, the raising of livestock, the building of great cities, the development of iron working, the forging of tools and the invention of musical instruments. Tragically, however, by chapter 6, the vast majority of humanity had chosen to turn their backs on God. (**Genesis 6:5-6**) There was one man, Noah, who had chosen to walk with God. (**Genesis 6:9**) Like all people, Noah was a sinner. Yet because He believed what God said, he was declared righteous: having all his sins forgiven and being fully accepted by God. He would no longer be treated as a sinner, but as a friend. What a contrast to the people who surrounded Noah. The world had become horrifically evil and violent as they vehemently rejected God.

Noah built the Ark by Faith:

Because God is holy and must punish sin, He told Noah He would send a judgment of floodwaters to destroy all life upon the earth. (**Genesis 6:13-14**) God gave Noah detailed instructions on how to build an ark in order to save all those who would believe, from the coming judgment. (**Genesis 6:14-16,22**) **Hebrews**

11:7 explains that Noah built the ark by faith. Faith is trusting that something is true even when you cannot see it. Even though Noah could not see the coming Flood, he built the ark trusting that what God said was true.

The Majority was Wrong:
According to **2 Peter 2:5**, Noah must have also been pleading with the people around him, urging them to trust what God had said. They, however, refused to believe. In the entire world, only eight people chose to follow God; Noah and his wife, and his three sons Shem, Ham and Japheth and their wives. (**Genesis 7:7**) So many times we tend to decide what we will believe about what is right and wrong based upon what the *majority* of the people around us think…but what about when the majority is wrong?

God Provided One way to be Saved:
It would have been impossible to ignore the fact that something divine was happening when God miraculously sent animals to the ark! (**Genesis 7:15-16**) Not only was God planning for the survival of each species, God was giving one last chance for the world to see the reality of the coming Flood! The end of verse 16 says, that after Noah and his family were safe inside the ark, God Himself shut the door! The time for choosing whether or not to follow God was over.

For those who had delayed their decision, it was too late. (**Genesis 7:11**) God's Word had really come to pass, and they realized they had rejected the truth! Although God had provided *one way* for them to be saved, they had turned their backs on God. (**Genesis 7:17-21**) Noah and his family were rescued from the flood not because they were not sinners, but because they had believed God. Just as God provided the ark as the only way to be saved from judgment, this event pointed to the future, and a day when God in His love, would provide *one way* for all of humanity to be saved.

The Story of Abraham:
Genesis 9-11 tell us that Noah lived for another 350 years after the Flood. It was during his son Shem's lifetime, only two years after Noah's death, that one of the most famous men in all of history was born: Abraham. **Genesis 12-25** records the history of Abraham's life. Abram, as he was first called, was a descendant of Shem. A rich man with many servants and flocks, Abram was married to Sarai, but they had no children because she was barren.

God's Promise to Abram:
In **Genesis 12:1-3**, God revealed a special plan that He had for Abram. First, God said He would be guiding Abram to a land that would be his and his descendants' future possession. Second, God would be birthing a

great nation through Abram. And third and most important, God promised that all people on earth would be blessed through him. (**Genesis 12:3**)

Because of sin, all people are under a curse of judgment. God promised a blessing for all people through Abram. This was because the coming Deliverer would be a physical descendant of Abram and bring blessing to all people, for He would come to free humanity from the curse of sin and death!

Abram Believed God's Promise:

Years later, God repeated His promise to give Abram a son. (**Genesis 15:4-6**) Verse 6 says that Abram, *"...believed the LORD."* When Abram put his faith in God's promise the rest of the verse tells us God, (**Genesis 15:6**) *"...credited it to him as righteousness."* Abram was declared to be righteous. But what had Abram done to deserve this? Abram hadn't given anything to God or performed any religious ceremony. He hadn't done any good works to merit this. God said Abram was righteous simply because he *believed* God's promise.

God Fulfills His Promise to Abram:

As the years went by, however, and Abram and Sarai remained childless, their situation seemed hopeless. **Genesis 16** tells us that Sarai convinced Abram to produce a child through Hagar, her Egyptian maidservant. Hagar gave birth to Ishmael. God graciously blessed Ishmael and caused a nation to descend from him as well. But Ishmael was not the son God had promised.

Finally, in **Genesis 17**, when Abram was 99 years old, the LORD appeared to Abram and told him that just as God had promised earlier, his wife, *Sarai*, would miraculously give birth to a son. (**Genesis 17:19**) On that same day, God changed their names to Abraham and Sarah. (**Genesis 17:5,15**) How exciting that year must have been as they dreamed of the day when they would hold their son, the son through whom the Deliverer would come. (**Genesis 21:1-2**)

The Worship of God:

As little Isaac grew up, Abraham surely taught him how to worship the Lord. Scripture tells us that one of the ways God's followers would worship Him, was through sacrifices. They would build an altar, and on this altar they would place an animal, often times a lamb. God's people realized they were sinners and that the payment for sin was death. The lamb was then killed and burned in God's presence. It was a sobering illustration of an innocent one dying in the place of those who were guilty.... dying that they might live.

The Unforgettable Sacrifice:

Although they must have offered many sacrifices to the LORD, both Isaac and Abraham were about to face a sacrifice neither of them would ever forget. In a divine test, God asked Abraham to offer his son, Isaac, as a sacrifice. (**Genesis 22:1-2**) Abraham had waited 25 years for this son! Would Isaac now have to die? Abraham did not understand what God was doing, but he determined to obey the LORD. (**Genesis 22:3-5**) Abraham realized that somehow God had a higher plan. For God had promised that a nation, and eventually the Deliverer, would come through Isaac. Therefore, based on God's promise, Abraham reasoned that perhaps God was planning to raise Isaac from the dead. (**Hebrews 11:17-19**) When they arrived in the region of Moriah, Abraham confidently told his servants that after he and Isaac offered the sacrifice, they would both return.

God Will Provide a Substitute:

As Abraham and Isaac climbed Mount Moriah, Isaac carried the very wood on which he would die. (**Genesis 22:6-8**) After they built an altar, Isaac was bound and placed on top of the wood on the altar. But when Abraham took the knife to slay his son, the angel of the LORD stopped him. (**Genesis 22:9-12**) Then Abraham looked up and saw a ram caught by its horns in a thicket. (**Genesis 22:13**) Abraham took the ram and sacrificed it instead of his son, Isaac.

The wood had been for Isaac. The knife and the fire had been for Isaac's death. At the last moment, however, in the face of certain death, God had provided a *substitute*. A substitute is one who takes the place of another. That day, the ram died in Isaac's place so that Isaac would live. As a reminder forever of what God had done, Abraham named the place, (**Genesis 22:14**) *"The LORD will provide"*. You would think that Abraham would have named it, "The LORD *has* provided." A future day was coming, however, when God would once again provide a Substitute. One would die in order that others might live. He would be the ultimate *provision*.

CHAPTER 3: PROVISION

PERSONAL & RELEVANT

Topic One: The choice to believe

Question: Were Noah and his family sinners? Why did Noah and his family live while the others perished? (See **Hebrews 11:7**) What does **II Peter 3:9** say about God?

_____

_____

Topic Two: One way to be saved

Question: The Flood was a divine judgment of cataclysmic nature, but it wasn't a death sentence for everyone. How did this same event also showcase God's gracious provision?

_____

_____

Topic Three: Facing certain death

Question: When Isaac lay upon the altar with a knife above him, he faced what seemed to be certain death. How is this a picture of our condition before God?

Hint: **Romans 3:23** *describes our condition before God and* **Romans 6:23** *tells us the payment for this is death.*

_____

_____

Why didn't Isaac die that day?

_____

_____

WHAT DOES THIS MEAN FOR *YOU*?

1. The choice to believe... is up to you.

"As Adam and Eve's descendants populated the earth, each of them had a choice to obey God or to reject Him. Noah and his family, chose to follow God while the rest of the world turned their backs on God becoming evil, violent and corrupt. Because God is holy and sin must be punished, God told Noah that He would send a judgment of floodwaters because of their wickedness. God in His love, however, provided one way to be saved from the Flood. All those who believed in what God said entered the ark. All those who refused, perished. In the same way, God must punish your sin, but God in His love has provided one way for you to be saved as well."

2. A blessing... for you.

"After the Flood, when the world began to be repopulated, God chose a man named Abraham to be the father of a nation. It was through this nation that the Deliverer would one day come. Through Him, all people on earth would be blessed. It was the promise of a blessing for you."

3. God provided a substitute... for you.

"In a divine test, God asked Abraham to offer Isaac as a sacrifice. But before Abraham could slay his son, God provided a substitute to die in his place! A ram died so that Isaac could live. Isaac is a picture of you! This day was pointing to a future event... a day when God would provide Someone who would die as a substitute for you."

CHAPTER 3: PROVISION

Read it for yourself:

Romans 3:23	All people are sinners
Romans 6:23	The payment for sin is death.
Genesis 6:9-22 and 7:1-34; 8:13-20	The Flood
Genesis 12:1-3	God's promise to Abraham
Genesis 21:1-3	Isaac is born.
Genesis 22: 1-14	The ram dies in Isaac's place.

Dig Deeper

Evidence for a Global Flood	**Pg. 136**
God does not want anyone to perish.	**II Peter 3:9**
What happens when wicked people repent.	**Jonah 3**

Memorize this:

"...*He is patient with you, not wanting anyone to perish, but everyone to come to repentance.*" **II Peter 3:9**

CHAPTER 4

DELIVERANCE

As God delivers His people from slavery He demonstrates that He alone is God. During the tenth plague, the only way to escape death points to a future deliverance of a world in bondage to sin and death.

Moses is Born:

As the years went by, Abraham's son, Isaac, had a son named Jacob. As an adult, God gave Jacob a new name and called him Israel. Israel had 12 sons. The families of these 12 sons grew into what became known as the 12 tribes of Israel. When a famine ravaged the land of Canaan, they went to live in Egypt. There, the children of Israel lived as strangers in a country that was not their own, and their nation grew.

Over time, a new ruling Pharaoh of Egypt feared that the Israelites might become too numerous and powerful, so Egypt enslaved them. (**Exodus 1:1-14**) In an attempt to control the Israelite population growth, Pharaoh ordered that every Israelite boy be thrown into the River Nile. (**Exodus 1:22**) At this tumultuous point in history, a baby named Moses was born to an Israelite family. (**Exodus 2:1-2**) In a series of providential events, God protected Moses' life, and he was adopted by Pharaoh's daughter. (**Exodus 2:3-10**)

Egypt Worshipped Many Gods:

Egypt had rejected the One true God and had exchanged the truth of God for a lie. They worshipped and served created things instead of the Creator. The Egyptians didn't worship God, who had created the River Nile, they worshipped the river itself, even offering a national sacrifice of a boy or a girl each year to appease Hapi, the Nile "god". They had a host of other false gods they worshipped: Heket, the frog headed goddess of life and birth, Hathor the cow goddess, Shu the god of the sky, and Amun-Re the sun god. Egypt's ruler, the Pharaoh, had gone so far as to declare himself to be a god-king.

Moses Chose to Follow the One True God:

For prince Moses, Egypt appeared to have everything: military might, influence, prestige and power. (**Acts 7:22**) Moses knew that there was only one true God, the Creator of the heavens and the earth. For Moses, following God and believing in His promise to send a Deliverer was of greater worth than all the treasures of Egypt. (**Hebrews 11:24-25**) Like Moses, you and I also have a choice to make. Following God may not be easy, but it will be of greater worth than all this world has to offer.

Moses Called to Deliver the Israelites:

Scripture tells us that one day, in an attempt to bring justice for the Israelites in his own strength, Moses killed an Egyptian, and as a result had to flee to the land of Midian where he lived as a shepherd. (**Exodus 2:11-15**) Though years passed, God however, had not forgotten His promise to His people. One day on Mt. Sinai[1], God called Moses to deliver the Israelites from slavery. (**Exodus 3:1-10**) God assured Moses that He would be with him and that He, Himself, would rescue His people and bring them out of Egypt to worship Him on that very mountain. (**Exodus 3:11-12**) "I AM" would be the name by which his people would know Him[2]. (**Exodus 3:14**) For God is not the "I Was", nor the "I Will Be". He is the "I AM", eternal, unchanging, and all-powerful.

Moses Demands the Release of the Israelites:

However, it would not be easy for Moses to face the Pharaoh and tell him that the LORD demanded the release of the slaves. God allowed Aaron, Moses' brother, to go with Moses into Pharaoh's presence. When confronted however, Pharaoh refused to release the slaves and was insulted that the God his slaves worshipped was telling him what to do! (**Exodus 5:2**) Pharaoh mocked God by asking: "Who is the LORD[3]?" His question was about to be answered by God Himself. (**Exodus 7:10-12**) In demonstration of God's power, Aaron threw down his staff and it became a snake, through the power of God.

Two Sources of Supernatural Power:

The Egyptian sorcerers also threw down their staffs and they turned into snakes. One may wonder *how* the sorcerers were capable of turning their staffs into snakes. According to the Bible, there are only two sources from which supernatural power is available: from God or from God's enemies, Satan and the demons. The Bible tells us that Satan is a liar and a deceiver. In his offer to people of solutions or power, he can often appear

---

[1] Mt. Sinai is also called Mt. Horeb or the "mountain of God"

[2] "I AM" is often translated in later passages of the in English versions of the Bible as "LORD"

[3] "The LORD" is the same name "I AM." Pharaoh was saying, "Who is this 'I AM' God telling me what to do?!"

harmless. Satan can even masquerade as an angel of light. However, his intentions are always to use people for his own evil purposes, and destroy them in the process. That is why the Bible strictly prohibits calling upon any force or power other than God. (**Deuteronomy 18:10-11**) God says that divination, sorcery, witchcraft, casting spells, being a medium or spiritist or other activities like these, are detestable. God urges us to put our confidence in Him alone! And in **Exodus 7:12** when God's staff swallows the sorcerers' staffs, God demonstrated that no power is greater than His power. God always has the victory!

The LORD Judged their False Gods:

Despite all of this, Pharaoh refused to listen to God. (**Exodus 7:13**) At that moment, God could have stretched out His hand with one plague, and simply wiped Egypt off the face of the earth. But He had other plans. **Exodus 7-12** describe a series of ten plagues that God brought upon Egypt. Each one demonstrated the power of God over the false gods of the Egyptians. (**Numbers 33:4**) God's heart was not only for the Israelites. (**Exodus 6:6-7**) He also wanted the Egyptians to know that He alone was the one true God. (**Exodus 7:5**) Each plague exposed to the Egyptians that the false gods in whom they trusted, were completely incapable of saving them.

One Way to Escape Death:

Pharaoh's heart remained hardened through the first nine plagues. As the tenth plague approached, the LORD explained to Moses what was about to take place. At midnight, the LORD would send the death angel to strike down the firstborn son of every household. (**Exodus 11:4-5**) There was only one way to escape death. If a year old[4], perfect, male lamb's blood was shed and placed on the doorposts of the home, God promised that He would not permit the Destroyer to enter that home and strike them down. (**Exodus 12:3-23**)

You Must Believe God's Message in order to be Saved:

What if that day someone heard God's message through Moses, but did not put blood on their doorway. Would simply knowing the truth be enough to save them? No. They had to also believe and apply the blood to their doorway. What if someone else decided that instead of the blood of the lamb, they would put a sign on their doorway that stated: "We are good people. We are religious. We give to the poor. We are law-abiding citizens." Would God be so impressed with their good deeds and spare them? No! Before God, only one factor determined whether the firstborn son lived or died. If a lamb, perfect and without blemish had died in his place, God said, (**Exodus 12:13**) *"When I see the blood I will pass over you."*

---

[4] A year old lamb was a young adult.

Slaves Set Free:

That night, the Israelites obeyed what the LORD had commanded Moses and Aaron, and lived. It was only after the Pharaoh had lost his oldest son that he released the Israelites. (**Exodus 12:28-31**) God's people would forever remember the events that led up to their deliverance: certain death, only one way to be saved, an innocent lamb dying so that they might live, no broken bones, shed blood, the power of the enemy broken… slaves set free! That night, about six hundred thousand men set out from Egypt, along with their families and also many other people. (**Exodus 12:37-38**) Surely, some of the Egyptians must have seen the futility of their false gods and chosen to believe the one true God who is LORD of all the earth.

Total Deliverance:

Yet, Pharaoh's heart became hardened once more. He sent his army in pursuit of the Israelites, where they overtook them as they were camped by the Red Sea. (**Exodus 14:5-9**) Unbeknownst to the Egyptians, this was also part of the sovereign plan of God. To the terror-stricken Israelites Moses said, (**Exodus 14:13-14**) "Do not be afraid. Stand firm and you will see the Deliverance the LORD will bring you today… The LORD will fight for you; you need only to be still."

As Moses stretched out his hand over the sea, the LORD drove back the sea with a strong east wind. All night the Israelites crossed the sea. When Pharaoh's army rushed after them into the sea, God threw their horses into confusion. When all the Israelites had safely crossed to the other side, Moses extended his hand out over the sea, and the waters flowed back and covered the Egyptian army; not one of them survived. (**Exodus 14:19-28**) The Israelites had now been totally freed from the bondage of the Egyptians, never to be enslaved by them again. The LORD had fought for them and had given them total Deliverance!

CHAPTER 4: DELIVERANCE

PERSONAL & RELEVANT

Topic One: Not an easy choice

Question: Moses chose to turn his back on all the power and pleasures that Egypt had to offer in order to follow God. This choice held obvious suffering and loss. Why would he would do that?

What are some possible consequences that people face today when they choose to follow God? Is it worth it?

_____

_____

Topic Two: Power from beyond this world

Question: What are the venues in which our culture encourages people to seek after other powers or forces? According to the Bible, if God is not the source of this power who is?

Spirit healings? Psychic readings? What examples can you think of?

_____

_____

Topic Three: Really bad? Really good? Did it make a difference?

Question: What if someone were an outstanding citizen, conscientious and responsible, (the type of person everyone wants for a neighbor!) but that person didn't put blood on their doorway during the last plague. What would happen?

Or, what about a reverse scenario: What if some jerk (who no one liked) put blood on his doorway, what would happen to him? What do you think God was showing His people that night?

_____

_____

WHAT DOES THIS MEAN FOR YOU?

1. The choice to follow God will be worth it for you.

"God miraculously preserved the life of a Hebrew baby named Moses. As an adult, he made a choice to follow the one true God. For Moses, this decision held possible suffering and loss. He realized however, that Egypt's pleasures were temporary, but the reward of following God would be eternal. Perhaps you also face a similar decision. The choice to follow God will be just as worth it for you, as it was for Moses."

2. God wants you to rely on Him alone.

"When Pharaoh refused to free the Israelite slaves, God demonstrated his power over the Egyptian gods in a series of supernatural events. When God turned Aaron's staff into a snake, Pharaoh's sorcerers also transformed their staffs into snakes. They did this by relying on the power of demons, or false gods. God then sent ten plagues on Egypt, each one showing that the false gods the Egyptians worshiped were completely incapable of saving them. Satan and the demons have always sought to entice people into invoking their power through sorcery, witchcraft, and divination, but God strictly prohibits this in his Word. When you need to turn to someone for help, remember that there is no power greater than the power of God. He loves you, and wants you to rely on Him alone."

3. The Lamb was a picture of a future Substitute for you.

"During the tenth plague, God sent the death angel to strike down the firstborn son of every household, but He also provided a way for the son to be saved. God said that if they took a perfect lamb, killed it and placed it's blood on their doors, the firstborn son would not die during the plague. The lamb became a substitute for those who believed God, and did as He instructed. These dramatic events were pointing to the future when God would provide a Substitute who would shed His blood for you, in order to give you eternal Deliverance."

Read it for yourself:

Exodus 1	The Israelites are slaves in Egypt.
Exodus 2	Moses is born and adopted by the princess.
Hebrews 11:24,25	Moses' choice to follow God
Exodus 7-11	Plagues on Egypt
Exodus 12	The Passover Lamb
Exodus 14	Crossing the Red Sea
Deuteronomy 18:10,11	God forbids seeking after other powers

Dig Deeper

Is there Demonic Activity in the World Today?	**Pg. 138**
What is the Christian View of Psychics or Fortune Tellers?	**Pg. 141**
Satan comes to steal, kill and destroy.	**John 10:10**
We are told to trust in God with all our hearts.	**Proverbs 3:5,6**

Memorize this:

"In Him we have redemption through His blood, the forgiveness of sins, in accordance with the riches of God's grace." **Ephesians 1:7**

CHAPTER 5

THE LAW

When God gives His holy laws at Mt. Sinai, the moral standard they reveal works like a mirror to show the sin within every human heart and drives people to realize that their only hope is in the coming Deliverer.

The Ten Commandments and God's Covenant:
God began to lead the Israelites to the land He had promised to Abraham. As they journeyed through the desert, God miraculously led the Israelites and provided food and water for them. After three months of traveling, they finally arrived at Mt. Sinai[5]; the mountain to which God had promised to bring Moses and the Israelites. There at Mt. Sinai, God made a covenant with the Israelites. The core terms of this covenant are known as the Ten Commandments. The terms of the covenant, or the Law, revealed more of God's character and His perfect standard of right and wrong. The Ten Commandments were inscribed on two tablets of stone by the very finger of God. The Israelites were required to perfectly obey all of God's laws. In response, they confidently told Moses, (**Exodus 19:8**) *"We will do everything the LORD has said."* But would they be able to keep the terms of the covenant and obey God's laws? As we look at these commands, ask yourself the same question. How many of these laws do you obey?

1: You shall have no other gods before me: Exodus 20:3
Exodus 20:1-2 reminds us that Israel had just left a country that believed there were a multitude of gods and goddesses to be served and appeased. But God's first commandment to His people was: (**Exodus 20:3**) *"You shall have no other gods before me."* God commanded His people to worship, trust, and serve Him alone. God explains that, (**Isaiah 45:5**) *"...[A]part from Me there is no [other] god."* Do you daily put your trust in God alone? What about when you are faced with a serious problem such as a sickness or a financial crisis; where do you go for help? Who or what do you seek after in order to gain guidance, protection, or prosperity? Or perhaps you have lived your whole life completely trusting in yourself? (**Jeremiah 17:5**) If you placed your

---

[5] Also known as Mt. Horeb, or the "Mountain of God"

trust in yourself or in any other being, spirit or source of power other than God, then you have broken this commandment.

2: You shall not make for yourself an idol: Exodus 20:4-6

God forbade His people from making an idol made to look like any heavenly being, angel or even God Himself. God also commanded them not to make idols in the form of animals, vegetation, or people; either living or dead. God also prohibited worshipping idols, bowing down to them or venerating them. (**Isaiah 42:8**) Have you ever given your praise to an idol or bowed down to it? Have you ever worshipped or prayed to an image? If so, you've broken this commandment. There are over 200 verses in the Bible against idolatry. Isaiah explains that those who are worshipping idols have had their hearts deceived without ever questioning, (**Isaiah 44:20**) *"Is not this thing in my right hand a lie?"* Over and over again, God commands His people to not trust in idols, (**Isaiah 46:5-10**) urging them, "I am God! I am your Creator! Worship, serve and trust Me alone!."

3: You shall not misuse the name of the Lord your God: Exodus 20:7

God's name is to be used with utmost honor. God prohibited His people from using His name in a curse or simply in an empty expression. Think about it. When someone says, "Oh my God, it is so hot today!" or " Oh my God, that is so awesome!", were they thinking about God or praying to Him? No! Have you ever used God's name as an expression? Have you ever blurted out God's name without even thinking about what you were saying? If you have, then you have broken this commandment.

4: Remember the Sabbath day by keeping it holy: Exodus 20:8-11

God commanded His people to not work on the seventh day of each week, but instead, dedicate that day to Him. Observance of this day not only gave His people a day of rest in which they could worship Him, but also uniquely set the nation of Israel apart from the other nations around them. Have you obeyed this law? If you are basing your acceptance by God on the fact that you keep the Sabbath, you need to realize failing to dedicate even one Sabbath to God means you have broken this commandment.

5: Honor your father and your mother: Exodus 20:12

God not only commanded us to obey our parents, but also to honor them. Honoring goes beyond outward conformity and deals with the heart. The opposite of honoring would include disobedience, talking back, arguing or being disrespectful. Have you ever done any of these things to your parents? If so, then you've broken this commandment.

6: You shall not murder: Exodus 20:13

God, as the Author and Giver of life, views every human being as precious. Many of us read the command to not murder and think, "Well, at least, this is one commandment that I've never broken! I've never killed anyone." Are you sure? Listen to these verses from **Matthew 5:21-22**: *"You have heard that it was said to the people long ago, 'Do not murder, and anyone who murders will be subject to judgment.' But I tell you that anyone who is angry with his brother will be subject to judgment."* All our actions flow from our hearts. God will judge not only the act of murder, but a heart with murderous thoughts. **1 John 3:15** says: *"Anyone who hates his brother is a murderer..."* Have you ever hated anyone, or been angry with them? If so, you've also broken this commandment.

7: You shall not commit adultery: Exodus 20:14

God is also the Author and Designer of marriage. From the very beginning, God intended marriage to be one woman for one man for a lifetime. In **Proverbs 5:18**, God tells the husband: *"...[R]ejoice in the wife of your youth."* In **Proverbs 5:19** He says: *"...[M]ay you ever be captivated by her love."* The physical intimacy that a husband and wife share is a precious gift to their marriage.

Adultery, is being sexually intimate with someone to whom you are not married. God says: "Don't do that! If you do, you'll destroy yourself, and your marriage!" Some people read this commandment and think, "I'm not even married, so I haven't broken this commandment." God demands all people to be pure, not only in their actions, but with their eyes and heart as well. **Matthew 5:28** says, *"...[A]nyone who looks at a woman lustfully has already committed adultery with her in his heart."* If you have looked in lust at the body of a person you are not married to, then you are guilty of breaking this commandment.

8: You shall not steal: Exodus 20:15

Stealing is taking anything that doesn't belong to you, but belongs to someone else. Have you ever cheated, taking answers that weren't rightfully yours? Have you ever taken music, movies, or information that you didn't pay for? Have you ever cheated on your taxes, or at your job, saying that you worked eight hours when you only worked seven? If under any circumstance you have taken something that does not belong to you, then you have broken this commandment.

9: You shall not give false testimony against your neighbor: Exodus 20:16

God only speaks the truth, and He requires that we also speak the truth in everything that we say. We have a tendency, however, to think, "Oh, it's just a little white lie; it's ok, nobody's going to get hurt." But **Matthew 12:36** says that all people, *"...[W]ill have to give account on the Day of Judgment for every careless word they have spoken."* Have you ever told a lie? If so, then you've broken this commandment.

10: You shall not covet: Exodus 20:17

Not only is coveting a sin, but it often leads a person to break other commands of God in order to get whatever it is they are coveting. What about you? Have you ever become dissatisfied with what you already have, and been consumed with the desire to have something that is not yours? If so, you've coveted and are guilty of breaking this commandment.

God will judge every single action:

The truth is, every single person who honestly evaluates their life will have to admit they have broken God's commandments. And like the Israelites, we have done it over and over again. We have a problem then because God is holy. He is completely pure with nothing evil in Him. He requires absolute obedience to these laws. God says, (**Galatians 3:10**) *"Cursed is everyone who does not continue to do everything written in the Book of the Law."*

What gives eternal magnitude to these commandments is the fact that God also says, (**Hebrews 9:27**) *"...[M]an is destined to die once and after that to face judgment."* Rich or poor, educated or not, good or bad, no one escapes death. After death, God will judge every single person. He knows all the careless words that you have spoken. He has taken note of of everything that your hands have done, and each place that your feet have gone. All the hidden secrets you thought no one knew were recorded by God. (**Revelation 20:12**) He will judge every single one of these actions.

The Law functions like a mirror:

In light of these sobering facts, the question begs to be asked: If God already knew that we wouldn't be able to obey His laws, *why* then did He give them to us? **Romans 3:20** explains, *"...[T]hrough the law we become conscious of sin."* The reason God gave us the Ten Commandments was so that we would realize we are sinners! God's holy laws functioned like a mirror showing the people their own sinfulness. When we look at the Law, we realize our own lives are full of evil.

The Law leads us to the Deliverer:

Galatians 3:24 says that God also gave the Law in order to lead people to the coming Deliverer! God knew if the people could recognize the fact they were sinners, they would realize they needed Someone to rescue them from their sins. The Deliverer would be the only One who would be able to perfectly obey God's laws. His life would be completely pure with nothing evil in Him. He would be the only One who would be able to resolve the problem of their sins. God knew, in order for the people to realize their only hope was in the coming Deliverer, they needed *the Law.*

CHAPTER 5: THE LAW

PERSONAL & RELEVANT

Topic One: Measuring up?

Question: What are some New Year's resolutions you have made in the past? Have you always been able to measure up to the standards *you* set for yourself? After watching this episode, *The Law*, do you feel like you've been able to measure up to *God's* standards?

_____
_____

Topic Two: Can the bad be balanced out by good?

Question: Is it possible to do enough good deeds to outweigh your bad ones?

If you cheated on a test but then walked out and bought a beggar some food, would that help settle the account with God?

*See **James 2:10**

_____
_____

Topic Three: Do you *really* think of yourself as that good?

Question: How would you feel about a movie that portrayed one week of your life, and in this movie it revealed every single action, word and thought you had during that week? What does **Hebrews 4:13** say?

_____
_____

WHAT DOES THIS MEAN FOR *YOU*?

1. You have broken God's laws.

"God required perfect obedience to His laws. Although the Israelites were confident they would be able to keep them, because of their sinfulness, they could not. They broke His Laws over and over again. An honest evaluation of your life will reveal that you also have broken God's commandments. Because of your sin, perfect obedience is also impossible for you."

2. You will have to give account to God.

"In Hebrews 9:27 it is written that "...[M]an is destined to die once and after that to face judgment." After death, God will judge every single person according to what they have done. Even if you have kept the whole law, and only broken one command, James 2:10 says that you are guilty of breaking all of it. The day will come when you will have to give account to God for every action, every word and every thought."

3. Someone to rescue you

"When God gave the people the Law, He already knew that they would not be able to keep His commandments. Like a mirror that reveals to us an imperfection, The Ten Commandments reveal to people the sin in their lives and hearts. The Law pointed people to the coming Deliverer. Their only hope would be in Someone who could rescue them from their sins.... this is the only hope for me and for you."

Read it for yourself:

Exodus 20:1-17	The Ten Commandments
James 2:10	Breaking one commandment condemns you
Isaiah 42:8	God will not share His glory with idols
Matthew 5:21-22	God judges hate like murder
Matthew 5:28	God judges lust like adultery
Revelation 20:12	Everyone will be judged by God.
Romans 3:20	The Laws makes us conscious of our sin.

Dig Deeper

God knows everything about us and we will give account to Him.	**Hebrews 4:13**
All of us have sinned.	**Romans 3:23**
If we say we have never sinned, we're lying!	**1 John 1:8**

Memorize this:

"...[N]o one will be declared righteous in God's sight by the works of the law; rather, through the law we become conscious of our sin." **Romans 3:20**

CHAPTER 6

ATONEMENT

The Day of Atonement, sacrifices, and a rebellious nation perishing from venomous snake bites, all serve to reveal how the coming Deliverer would be the innocent One dying in order that others might live.

God's Plan of Atonement:

Until the Deliverer came, God continued to reveal a way in which His people could be forgiven, and not receive the punishment they deserved for their sins. There, at Mt. Sinai, God not only gave His people the Law, but God also revealed to Moses His plan of Atonement. Atonement is the turning aside of God's punishment. Instead of pouring out His punishment upon the sinful people, God would provide a way in which His punishment would be turned aside.

Atonement was made at the Tabernacle:

All the requirements for atonement were to be performed at a magnificent, portable structure called the Tabernacle. At the Tabernacle, God manifested His presence by a cloud that came to rest above the Tabernacle. Later on, the Tabernacle would be replaced by a permanent structure called the temple. But until that day came, the Tabernacle would be the center of all activity concerning atonement. God also chose men called priests to represent the nation in fulfilling the requirements that God had instituted. The priests were the ones who were to now bring the offerings and sacrifices to God at the Tabernacle, and the leader of the priests was called the high priest.

A Perfect Substitute:

When the Israelites came to the Tabernacle to make atonement for their sins, they weren't to offer just any animal. God gave them very specific instructions. (**Leviticus 1:2-3**) All animals offered to the Lord were to be perfect, they with no defects. This was to symbolize the moral perfection that God required. Notice that when a man offered a sacrifice, the man was not inspected for perfection. (**Leviticus 1:3**) No one asked him, "Have you been saying prayers? Have you been helping the poor? Have you been a good citizen?" No! The man was not examined; the man was a sinner! Rather, the animal was examined, and had to be found perfect. The *animal* was examined in the man's place as his substitute.

God's Punishment Turned Away from the Sinner:

The man would then place his hand on the head of the animal. (**Leviticus 1:4**) By this action he was admitting, "I am a sinner, but I am bringing this animal as my substitute to die in my place." Then **Leviticus 1:4** continues: *"...[I]t will be accepted on his behalf to make atonement for him."* To the man, God was saying: "Because this animal is taking your punishment in your place, I will turn my punishment away from you." Since the payment for sin is death, that animal was then killed, instead of the man. Its blood was shed. In **Hebrews 9:22** God says that, *"...without the shedding of blood there is no forgiveness."* And in **Leviticus 17:11** God also explains, *"For the life of a creature is in the blood, and I have given it to you to make atonement for yourselves on the altar..."* A life had been given in the place of another. And when God saw the blood of the sacrifice, His punishment was turned away from the man because a substitute had taken his place. This is how atonement, the turning aside of God's punishment, was made for an individual.

Atonement for the Entire Nation:

There was a special day every year in which Atonement was to be made for the sins of the entire nation. This day was called the Day of Atonement. (**Leviticus 16:34**) This was to take place in the Tabernacle. The Tabernacle was divided into two rooms: the Holy Place and the Most Holy Place. Within the Most Holy Place was a golden box containing the Ten Commandments, called the Ark of the Covenant. Inside this box were God's holy laws, the covenant that he had made with them. The Ark of the Covenant had a lid called the Atonement Cover. It was here that God promised His people that His presence would fill the Most Holy Place.

(**Leviticus 16:2**) A thick, multi-layered, richly embroidered curtain hung between the Holy Place and the Most Holy Place, blocking access to the Most Holy Place. With this curtain, God was showing the people that sinful man is separated from Holy God. No one was allowed behind the curtain into the Most Holy Place. God had warned them that if anyone went behind the Curtain into God's presence, they would surely die.

The Blood of the Substitute over the Law that Condemns

On the Day of Atonement, however, someone did go behind the curtain, into the Most Holy Place. (**Hebrews 9:7**) Every person in the nation had sinned and because the payment for sin is death, they all deserved to die.

On that day, the High Priest represented the entire nation. Once behind the curtain, the High Priest faced the Ark of the Covenant. Inside of the Ark of the Covenant were the Ten Commandments, God's holy laws, the laws the people were unable to keep, the laws that showed their complete sinfulness. In **Leviticus 16:15**, God commanded the High Priest to take the blood of the sacrifice, and sprinkle it on the Atonement Cover, and in front of it. There, above the Atonement Cover, was the presence of God, and beneath Him, were the laws that condemned them. But now, in between Holy God and sinful man, was the blood of the sacrifice; the innocent one that had died in the place of those who were guilty. When God looked down, instead of seeing the Law that condemned them, He chose to see the blood of the one who had died for them, as their substitute. And in this way, God's punishment was turned away from the people, and atonement was made.

Illustrations of a Future Atonement:

Through the sacrifices, God turned His punishment away from the people. These sacrifices, however, did not take away their sins. Rather, day after day, and year after year, they were a constant reminder of how sinful the people were! **Hebrews 10:1** explains that these sacrifices were only a shadow of the good things that were coming, and not the realities themselves. You see, although the people may not have understood it at the time, every sacrifice was a picture in God's eternal Plan of Salvation. Each time an animal's blood was shed, it pointed to a day in the future when blood would be shed to turn away God's punishment *once and for all.* Every time an animal was offered as a sacrifice, it pointed to a future day when One who was Innocent would come and die in the place of all those who were guilty, a day when atonement would be made not only for the sins of the nation, but for the sins of the whole world.

Rebellion in the Desert:

When the Israelites reached the border to the Promised Land, there was an uprising against God. Because of their lack of trust in God's power, the Israelites refused to enter the land, and instead demanded to go back to Egypt. God declared that, as a result of their disobedience, only their children would be allowed to enter the Land. God then led them back into the desert, where they were to wander for forty years until their children were old enough to enter the Promised Land, and the older generation that had refused to enter the land, had passed away.

Numbers 21 describes an important event which took place during these forty years in the desert. God had carefully led his people through the desert, protected them from all harm, and daily provided the food and water they needed. Yet, **Numbers 21:5** says that the people, ungrateful for all of God's provision, spoke against God and against Moses. In the face of this rebellion against God, God caused a series of dramatic events that would not only be recorded in Israel's history, but would be used by God to paint another striking picture of His eternal Plan of Salvation.

God Offered Life to the Entire Rebellious Nation:

Because of the people's rebellion against Him, **Numbers 21:6** says, *"Then the LORD sent venomous snakes among them; they bit the people and many Israelites died."* There was no cure for the snakebite, no hospitals, no medicine that would reverse the effects of the venom. All who were bitten would surely die. When the Israelites realized the peril they were in, they confessed their rebellion and cried out for help. (**Numbers 21:7**) In response to the people's cry for deliverance, God was about to provide complete healing. Not only would this healing reverse the effects of the poison, it would be offered freely by God. Life instead of death would be offered by God to every single person in the nation, regardless of age, gender, social status or even past rebellion against Him.

An Opportunity to Trust God:

In **Numbers 21:8-9**, we read that in obedience to God's instructions, Moses fashioned a snake out of bronze and hung it up on a pole. This snake was not to be an idol to be worshiped. Throughout the Bible, God strictly prohibits the worshiping of idols. Nor did this bronze snake have any magical powers. The reason God told Moses to place this snake on a pole was to give the people an opportunity to trust Him. The healing that God would provide would not be forced upon anyone. Every single person would have to *choose* whether they would accept or reject the healing God offered.

Trust, Look, Live:

God told Moses to announce to the people, (**Numbers 21:8**) *"...[A]nyone who is bitten can look at it and live."* When someone believed what God said, and looked at that snake on the pole, that person would instantly be healed and given life.

What if that day someone in the crowd said, "What?! That's all I have to do...just look?! No, that's too easy. That just seems too simple. I can't believe that. I'm not going to look." What would you say to that person? I would say, "Stop being prideful! Just look! Believe what God says; trust Him!"

What if someone else said, "I don't think it's necessary for me to look. I'm a very good person. I really think that God will see my heart and all of my good works, and heal me!" Do you think that's true? Would God heal them simply because they were a good person? No! It did not matter how good a person was! If they refused to look, then that person would die!

Lastly, what if someone else said, "I would like to look, I really would, but the problem is I'm not sure how my family and friends will react. They have already decided they are not going to look, so what will they think of me if I do? Because of this, I've decided not look either." What would you say? I would say, "Friend, I am so sorry that the others around you are choosing to reject life! You, though, can still choose life! You do not have to reject life because of them! This is your only hope!"

God will Always Do what He Says:

That day in the desert, thousands stood between life and death. They all had the same choice to make: Do I trust what God said and look, or do I refuse to listen to Him and die? **Numbers 21:9** says, *"When anyone was bitten by a snake and looked at the bronze snake, he lived."* God will always do what He says. You can trust His Word. Unbeknownst to the people that day, was the fact that in the same way that Moses had lifted up the snake in the desert, a day was coming when, like the bronze snake, the coming Deliverer would also be lifted up. This event in the desert pointed to a future day when those who faced eternal death would be given the choice to not receive the punishment for their sins, but instead accept eternal life.

PERSONAL & RELEVANT

Topic One: Examination

Question: At the time a sacrifice was offered, the priest had to make sure that there was perfection. Who or what was the priest examining? Why do you think this is significant?

_____

_____

Topic Two: Death on behalf of someone else

Question: Why the bloodshed? Why did God instruct them to sacrifice an animal on their behalf?

Wouldn't it have been shocking to participate in something like this and see a living thing killed?

*See **Leviticus 17:11**

_____

_____

Topic Three: The Most Holy Place

Answer the following questions:

Where did God manifest His presence in the Most Holy Place? (**Exodus 25:21,22**)

_____

What was the most significant item placed inside the Ark of the Covenant? (**Deuteronomy 10:4,5**)

_____

On the Day of Atonement, what was sprinkled on the lid of the Ark of the Covenant? (**Leviticus 16:14**)

_____

Why is this significant?

_____

Topic Four: Reasons to not believe?

Question: When God offered healing in the desert to all those bitten by the venomous snakes, we saw three hypothetical scenarios of people rejecting His offer of life.

Think through each one of the following excuses someone might have for not looking at the bronze serpent. How do they reveal a faulty perspective?

1. "It's too easy, so I'm not going to do it."
2. "I'm such a good person, surely God will accept me because of that."
3. "My friends and family are not going to look so I'm not either."

_____

_____

WHAT DOES THIS MEAN FOR *YOU*?

1. Examined in your place.

"When a man brought a sacrifice, instead of examining the man, the priest examined the lamb. The man who brought the lamb was a sinner who had broken God´s laws and could not please Him. It was the lamb who had to be found perfect, with no defects. In the same way, God knew that you would break His laws. That's why He already planned to send the Deliverer: He would live the perfect life and be examined by God in your place."

2. An Innocent One for you.

"After being examined, the lamb was then killed. The man was guilty, yet it was the lamb who died. In this way, God allowed His punishment to be turned away from the man. Each time a sacrifice was offered, an innocent one died in the place of the guilty. Every death pointed to the ultimate sacrifice that would be made in order to resolve the problem of your sin."

3. Atonement for you.

"Once a year, on the Day of Atonement, when the High Priest entered God's presence, the blood of the sacrifice was sprinkled on the Atonement Cover. Instead of condemning the nation, God chose to see the blood of the one who had died for them, and turned away His punishment

This too was pointing to a future day when blood would be shed for the forgiveness of the entire world. A day when God would provide atonement for you."

4. A life for you.

"During a rebellion against God in the desert, poisonous snakes were sent to bite the people. God provided a way that all those who were bitten could live. They had only to look at the bronze snake and they would be healed. Just as the snake bite was fatal, you too have a fatal condition called sin. When God provided a way for the people to live, this was a picture of the salvation God would offer the world, life He would offer to you."

Read it for yourself:

Leviticus 16:2	God's presence in the Tabernacle.
Leviticus 1:1-4	How sacrifices were brought.
Hebrews 9:7	Only the high priest could enter the Holy Place on the Day of Atonement.
Hebrews 10:1-3	These sacrifices could not take away their sins but only reminded them of how sinful they were. (Only the Deliverer would be able to fully pay for their sins.)
Numbers 21:1-9	The bronze snake.

Dig Deeper

Forgiveness could only take place because of the shedding of blood — **Hebrews 9:22**

Memorize this:

"...He was pierced for our transgressions, He was crushed for our iniquities; the punishment that brought us peace was on Him..." *Isaiah 53:5*

CHAPTER 7

LAMB OF GOD

God Himself takes on human form and comes to be the Deliverer, Jesus. As an adult, Jesus is proclaimed to be the Lamb of God who would take away the sins of the world.

The Eyewitness Accounts Spread like Wildfire:

The Roman Empire chose Greek to be the common language of communication for the entire empire. In 150 B.C., when God's Word was translated into the Greek language, everyone who could read Greek was able to read the prophecies about the Messiah, the Deliverer. With myriads of people now connected and speaking a common language, news never traveled so quickly. What took place next spread like wildfire across the empire, and changed the world forever. These events were carefully documented by eyewitnesses in four different books. These four books became known as the *euangelion*, which in Greek means Gospels, or "good news", and this is the message they carried.

Mary and Joseph were Waiting for the Promised Deliverer:

Within the Roman Empire, in the nation of Israel, in a small town called Nazareth lived a young lady named Mary. **Matthew 1:18** says that, "*Mary was pledged to be married to Joseph.*" Both she and her fiancé Joseph were devoted followers of God. **Matthew 1:19** says that Joseph was a righteous man, which is the word used to describe someone who has had their sins forgiven by God. **Luke 2:24** records Mary herself bringing an offering for her sins, and in **Luke 1:47**, Mary says, "*...[M]y spirit rejoices in God my Savior...*" Mary knew that she needed a Savior, and both she and Joseph, along with all those in Israel who loved God, surely must have longed for the coming of the Deliverer, their Messiah.

Jesus was Born of a Virgin:

Luke 1:26 says that God sent the angel Gabriel to deliver an important message to Mary. (**Luke 1:30-32**) The angel told Mary, who was a descendant of David, that she would give birth to a Son, named Jesus. He would reign forever and His kingdom would never end. This was the fulfillment of the prophecies given over a thousand years earlier when God promised that a descendant of King David would be the Messiah! (**2 Samuel 7:16**) This was the moment Israel had been waiting for!

When God chose a virgin, (**Luke 1:34-38**) a woman who had never had sexual relations with a man, to be the mother of the Messiah, God was also fulfilling the first promise He had given to Adam and Eve concerning the Deliverer who would be born without a human father! (**Genesis 3:15**) Matthew records that, (**Matthew 1:22**) *"All this took place to fulfill what the Lord had said through the prophet: 'The virgin will be with child and will give birth to a son, and they will call him Immanuel' - which means, 'God with us.' "*

Jesus' Divine Origin is Confirmed to Joseph:

Mary must have felt so honored to be the one who would carry the Messiah, but it wasn't going to be easy. In Israel at that time, if an unmarried woman became pregnant she faced public shame, rejection, and even possible death. Surely everyone in the small town of Nazareth talked about pregnant Mary. Joseph must have felt so betrayed and confused. Joseph had never had relations with Mary; he knew the child was not his. Joseph was considering quietly cutting off their engagement when God intervened by sending the angel, Gabriel, to explain to Joseph in a dream who the baby within Mary was! (**Matthew 1:20-21**) Imagine how Joseph felt when he realized that the baby inside Mary was to grow up to be their Messiah, the One who would save them from their sins! **Matthew 1:24** says that Joseph obeyed God, and immediately, *"…took Mary home as his wife."*

After Jesus was born, Joseph and Mary would enjoy the normal physical intimacy that a husband and wife share. Together they would have other children, whose names are listed for us in **Matthew 13:55** and mentioned in various other places in the Bible. Until Mary gave birth to Jesus, however, **Matthew 1:25** says of Joseph that, *"He had no union with her until she gave birth to a son."*

Jesus Born in Bethlehem:

After Mary and Joseph got married, they received more unexpected news. A Roman census was taken, ordering each citizen to return to their hometown to register. (**Luke 2:1-4**) It seemed so untimely for a pregnant woman to leave her home in Nazareth and travel roughly 80 miles[6] to Bethlehem, the town of their ancestors.

---

[6] 80 miles is 130 kilometers

This too, however, was part of God's perfect plan. 600 years earlier, God had given a prophecy found in **Micah 5:2** stating that the Messiah would be born in the town of Bethlehem.

There in Bethlehem, the promised Messiah was finally born, and yet the world was too busy or too preoccupied to even notice. (**Luke 2:6-7**) Instead of a palace, the King who was to reign forever was laid to sleep in a feeding trough. He came in a way that no one expected, in the silence of the night, in the care of peasants, in the humblest of settings.

Jesus is the Savior for All People:

(**Luke 2:8**) *"And there were shepherds living out in the fields nearby, keeping watch over their flocks at night."* The shepherds outside of Bethlehem were most likely tending the very sheep that were used for the sacrifices. Little did they realize that on that very night, the One who would save them from their sins had been born so that they would no longer need any sacrifices! God in His sovereignty chose to allow these shepherds to be the first ones to hear the announcement of the angels that the Savior, the Messiah, had been born! (**Luke 2:9-11**) The angels declared that this good news was to be for all people. Jesus had come to be the Savior for all of humanity. When the angels left them, the shepherds hurried off to Bethlehem and found the baby lying in a manger. (**Luke 2:15-16**)

Jesus is God:

He was, however, no ordinary baby. The One who had spoken the stars into existence had come to the earth as a human, and lay sleeping in a manger. The Bible clearly teaches that Jesus is God (**Philippians 2:6-7**) In order to be the Messiah, He became a servant; He came down to earth as a human. **Hebrews 2:14** and **John 1:14,18** affirm that the One who made the world, entered the world as a human. The Creator became a part of His creation.

Jesus Can Sympathize with Us:

Eventually Mary and Joseph did move back to Nazareth. Other than one story that took place when Jesus was twelve, (**Luke 2:41-50**) the Bible is silent about Jesus' childhood and growing up years. The Bible clearly states that although Jesus is God, during the first 30 years of his life here on earth, He did not perform any miracle, or display His power as God. Why did He do it? Why did He live such a simple life?

According to **Hebrews 4:15-16**, one of the reasons Jesus did this was so that we would be able to come to Him for help in our time of need, knowing that Jesus can sympathize with us. Whether it was going to school, growing up in a family, having parents misunderstand Him, or working hard to survive, He experienced all of the things that you and I go through. He wore our sandals and walked the dusty streets of our earth… for you and me.

John the Baptist Prepared the People for the Messiah:

(**Matthew 3:1**) John the Baptist was a messenger sent by God, to prepare the people for the Messiah. **Matthew 3:2** says he urged the people saying, "R*epent, for the kingdom of heaven is near."* Repent: this word in the Greek literally means to change your mind. You see, many people mistakenly thought that God would automatically accept them into Heaven because of their nationality, their good works, or their religious ceremonies. This perspective was wrong.

The Bible shows us in the Ten commandments that we have broken God's holy laws and are all guilty as sinners. John told the people that they needed to repent, in other words, to change their minds, and realize they were *not* good enough to get to Heaven. They needed to admit they were sinners, and needed a Savior.

(**Matthew 3:6**) Those who agreed with John's message demonstrated this by being baptized in the Jordan River. This baptism did not save them, nor did it wash away their sins. Rather, this baptism was an outward act that showed they agreed with John's message, believed they were sinners, and were looking forward to the coming Messiah.

John the Baptist Revealed that Jesus was the Messiah:

When Jesus was about thirty years old, the time came for the rest of the world to know that He was the Messiah. John the Baptist had been sent to prepare people's hearts for the Messiah, and also to reveal the Messiah to the nation. According to **John 1:33**, God told John that the man on whom he saw the Holy Spirit visibly descend, would be the Messiah. (**Mark 1:9**) When Jesus came to be baptized by John, it was not because He was sinful, but so that John could recognize Him as the Messiah. (**Mark 1:10-11**)

Jesus is Sinless:

As the Spirit descended upon Jesus, the Father audibly proclaimed that He was well pleased with Jesus. You see, all the other people who stood there that day were sinners; they could not please God. Amongst them, however, stood Jesus. He was the only one who could perfectly obey all of God's commands and fully please Him.

If Jesus was not sinless He would not be able to the Savior, the Messiah. The fact that Jesus was sinless was proven when He was led to the desert to be tempted by Satan. (**Mark 1:12-13**) Just as Satan had tempted

Adam and Eve to sin, Satan tempted Jesus. Unlike Adam and Eve, however, Jesus was victorious and did not give in to Satan's temptations and sin.

Throughout Jesus' life, Jesus was faced with all of the same temptations that you and I also face. **Hebrews 4:15** says that He was, "...*tempted in every way, just as we are - yet was without sin.*" **Luke 1:35** says that He is the "Holy One"; which means He is completely pure with nothing evil in Him. Only Jesus could fully please God. Only Jesus could live a perfect life, and not sin.

Jesus is the Lamb of God:

In the Old Testament, God instructed His people on how to bring animals as sacrifices for their sins. The man who brought the lamb was not examined. He was a sinner, not acceptable to God. As the man's substitute, however, the *lamb* had to be perfect; it could have no defects. The lamb was examined in the man's place.

In the same way that God allowed the lamb to be examined, Jesus came to be examined in our place, to be our Substitute. As Jesus was returning from the desert, victorious over sin and Satan, **John 1:29** says, "*[J]ohn saw Jesus coming toward him and said, "Look, the Lamb of God, who takes away the sin of the world!"* Jesus came to be the Lamb of God, to take our place, to be our Substitute.

God knew that you and I would fail, that we would sin. He knew that we could not perfectly obey His laws. He knew that we would need a substitute. Jesus came to be that substitute. Jesus came to live the life that you and I could not live. Jesus came to be the *Lamb of God*.

PERSONAL & RELEVANT

Topic One: Relatability

Question: Why do people who have been through similar experiences seem to share a connection? How would Jesus coming to earth to become human help us be able to relate to Him?

Have you ever heard women exchanging pregnancy stories, or war veterans talking? Why do they feel they can relate to each other? *Philippians 2:6,7*

_____

_____

Topic Two: Examined in your place

Question: We are incapable of perfectly keeping God's laws. What about Jesus, though? What are the implications of Jesus being called the "Lamb of God"?

If you had to take an extensive written exam, then found out an expert on the subject would be allowed to take the exam in your place, would you feel relieved? What if you had to run a race, then had the Olympic Gold medalist offer to run in your place for you?

_____

_____

Topic Three: Coincidence?

Question: Could the fulfillment of prophecies have been coincidence or manipulation? *(You will be looking at the article in your Appendix called: Messianic Prophecies & Fulfillments Pg. 143)*

_____

_____

CHAPTER 7: LAMB OF GOD

WHAT DOES THIS MEAN FOR *YOU*?

1. A Savior for you.

"When God sent an angel to proclaim to a virgin that she would give birth to the Messiah, this was the fulfillment of the first promise that had been given to Adam and Eve. God had told them a Savior would be born without a human father who would grow up and crush Satan's head. Jesus is this Promised Savior that all of the prophets had written about and that the people had awaited, for so many years. He is a Savior for you."

2. Out of love for you.

"The Messiah came in a way no one expected. For God Himself had come down to earth in human form. As Jesus grew up, He experienced all the joys and sorrows of the people he lived among. The Creator became a part of His creation... out of love for you."

3. A Lamb for you.

"God the Father, announced that Jesus was His beloved Son; the only One who could fully please God. Only Jesus could face Satan's temptations and live a perfect life and not sin. Jesus had come to be the perfect Lamb of God who takes away the sin of the world. Jesus came to be examined by God in your place; to be a substitute for you."

Read it for yourself:

Matthew 1:18-25; **Luke 1: 26-37; 2:1-21**	Jesus' birth
Philippians 2:6,7	Jesus took on human form to be born.
Matthew 3:1-6	John the Baptist tells people to repent.
Mark 1:9-11	Jesus is baptized. God declares Jesus to be the One who fully pleases Him.
Hebrews 4:15	Jesus was tempted in every way but did not sin.
John 1:29	Jesus is declared to be the Lamb of God.

Dig Deeper

Messianic Prophecies and Fulfillments	**Pg. 143**
Did the writers of the New Testament just copy from mythology?	**Pg. 146**
The Gospels are eyewitness accounts	**Luke 1:1-4**
Jesus became flesh to share in our humanity.	**Hebrews 2:14**

Memorize this:

"...John saw Jesus coming toward him and said, "Look, the Lamb of God, who takes away the sin of the world!"
John 1:29

CHAPTER 8

MESSIAH

With supernatural power over demons, sickness, nature and death itself,
Jesus proves that He is not only the Messiah but God Himself.
He reaches out to all people with a love unlike any other

Jesus Chooses 12 Disciples:

After Jesus' baptism and temptation He chose 12 men to accompany Him. These men were known as disciples, a word which simply means "learner". If you or I would have designated disciples, we would have probably appointed men who had fame, wealth, and power, people who were respected in all of society. Jesus didn't do that. Jesus sees people differently than we do. Some of the men that Jesus chose as disciples were common fishermen. One was a zealot, a member of a political party that opposed the Romans, and yet another man worked for the Romans as a tax collector! As Jesus reached out across all social, ethnic, and racial barriers, His disciples were willing to leave everything in order to follow Him.

Jesus Proclaims Himself the Messiah:

Jesus began to teach on the Sabbath in synagogues. (**Luke 4:14-15**) Synagogues were buildings in which the Israelites, or Jews, met to worship God. Different men took turns reading passages, and explaining them from God's Word. **Luke 4:16-17** tells us that while Jesus was at the synagogue in Nazareth, He selected a prophecy that had been written over 700 years earlier. (**Isaiah 61:1-2**) It was a prophecy concerning the Anointed One, the Messiah. (**Luke 4:18-19**) After reading this, the eyes of everyone in the room were on Him; what He said next astounded them: *"Today this scripture is fulfilled in your hearing."* (**Luke 4:21**) Jesus proclaimed that He was the fulfillment of that prophecy; He was the Anointed One they had been waiting for! Jesus announced that He was the Messiah.

Miracles Authenticated Jesus' Claim:

Perhaps you may be thinking, "Well, anyone can claim to be the Messiah, and anyone can say they're God, but is there any proof?" As you examine Jesus' life in the four biographies written about Him, you will find that Jesus did phenomenal things that no ordinary human being could do; these are called "miracles." Never once did Jesus use His supernatural power for His own personal comfort. Rather, these miracles were evidence given to back up His claim that He was the Messiah. **John 10:24-25** records that Jesus asserted that the miracles He performed authenticated His message, and proved to the watching world that Jesus was who He claimed to be.

Power and Authority over Demons:

Jesus' life was characterized by a divine power and authority over the spirit world. The Bible tells of instances where demons have caused muteness, blindness or even insanity. Demons have caused people to mutilate themselves, live like uncontrollable animals, or kill themselves.

We are first given a glimpse of Jesus' power over demons in a town called Capernaum, at a meeting in their synagogue. (**Mark 1:23-24**) The demon knew that because Jesus was the Holy One, He had the power to destroy him. When the man possessed by the demon cried out, Jesus gave orders to the the demon, "Be quiet!" (**Mark 1:25**) Then, as the entire synagogue watched in astonishment, Jesus commanded the evil spirit, (**Mark 1:25-27**) *"Come out of him!"* The people were astounded that Jesus Himself had the power to make the demon obey. Jesus did not have to call out to a higher power, or perform some ceremony to try to appease or manipulate the demon. Jesus had absolute power and authority over demons. He was fulfilling the prophecies that the Messiah would proclaim freedom for the prisoners and release the oppressed.

Power Over Sickness

Another most prominent aspect of Jesus' ministry was His power over sickness. **Matthew 15:30-31** says, *"Great crowds came to Him, bringing the lame, the blind, the crippled, the mute and many others, and laid them at His feet; and He healed them."* This power over sickness was one more proof that Jesus was indeed the promised Messiah. **Matthew 8:16-17** reports that Jesus, *"…[H]ealed all the sick. This was to fulfill what was spoken through the prophet Isaiah: 'He took up our infirmities and carried our diseases.'"*

Incredible Compassion and Love:

Jesus healed men, women, young, and old. They were not crowds to Jesus. Each person had a face and each face had a name, and He knew each one. Jesus reached out to the needy, the hurting and the outcast. He demonstrated a love and compassion like none the world has ever seen. Once, a man with leprosy, an incurable, infectious disease, came to Jesus and begged Jesus to heal Him. Unlike the others, Jesus did not run from him, nor did he recoil in disgust. Rather, **Mark 1:41** says, *"Filled with compassion, Jesus reached out his hand and touched the man."* Immediately, the man was completely healed! Jesus came to embrace the rejected, to heal the broken, and to touch the untouchable.

Jesus Feeds over 5000

Once, when Jesus was surrounded by a large crowd, **Mark 6:34** says that, *"...[H]e had compassion on them, because they were like sheep without a shepherd. So he began teaching them many things."* **Mark 6:35-38** goes on to recount that later that day Jesus asked His disciples to give the crowd something to eat. Jesus then directed them to go out amongst the crowd and see how much food was there. Two disciples came back and gave Jesus five loaves of bread and two fish.

"Taking the five loaves and the two fish and looking up to heaven, He gave thanks and broke the loaves. Then He gave them to His disciples to set before the people. He also divided the two fish among them all." (**Mark 6:41**) Afterward, *"...[T]he disciples picked up twelve basketfuls of broken pieces of bread and fish."* (**Mark 6:43**) that were leftover! *"The number of those who ate was about five thousand men, besides women and children."* (**Matthew 14:21**)

"After the people saw the miraculous sign that Jesus did, they began to say, 'Surely this is the Prophet who is to come into the world.'" (**John 6:14**) God had promised that the Messiah would be a prophet. (**Deuteronomy 18:18**) The prophet Moses had come to give them the words of God and set them free. As the fulfillment to this prophecy, Jesus had also come to give them the very words of God and set them free from the powers of sin, death, and hell.

Power over Death:

In **Revelation 1:18** Jesus said, *"I hold the keys of death."* Jesus demonstrated this power over death on several occasions. He had complete power over death itself. Once, when Jesus was nearing the city of Nain, **Luke 7:12** says, *"…[A] dead person was being carried out - the only son of his mother, and she was a widow."* This widow was heartbroken over the loss of her son, but Jesus had come to bring hope to the hopeless. *"When the Lord saw her, His heart went out to her and He said, 'Don't cry.' He went up and touched the bier, and those carrying it stood still. He said, 'Young man, I say to you, get up!' The dead man sat up and began to talk, and Jesus gave him back to his mother."* (**Luke 7:13-15**)

The One who had breathed life into the first man in the Garden, had now spoken life into this dead man. Those in the funeral procession, *"…were all filled with awe and praised God. 'A great prophet has appeared among us,' they said. 'God has come to help His people.'"* (**Luke 7:16**) Indeed, God had come; just as the Scriptures had foretold: *"…[T]hey will call Him Emmanuel – which means, 'God with us.'"* (**Matthew 1:23**)

Power over the Physical World:

One thing the disciples soon realized was that Jesus had complete power and authority over everything in the physical world. **John 6** describes for us a terrifying storm that the disciples faced alone. The disciples went ahead in their boat and left Jesus behind on a mountainside to spend time alone in prayer with the Father. That night the disciples battled the wind and the waves and only made it halfway across the lake. They were exhausted and without hope.

In the middle of the storm they looked up and *"…[T]hey saw Jesus approaching the boat, walking on the water; and they were terrified. But He said to them, 'It is I; don't be afraid.' Then they were willing to take Him into the boat, and immediately the boat reached the shore where they were heading."* (**John 6:19-21**) *"Then those who were in the boat worshiped Him, saying, 'Truly you are the Son of God.'"* (**Matthew 14:33**)

The disciples realized only God can calm a storm. Only God can give orders to the wind and the waves. Only God can walk on water. Only God is worthy of our worship.

Jesus is God:

As you examine the four biographies written about Jesus, you will find that his life demonstrated that He was in fact God. In the Old Testament, when God described Himself to His people, He used such terms as: King, Judge, Light, Rock, Redeemer, Creator, the Giver of Life, the One who Speaks with Divine Authority, and the One who has the Ability to Forgive Sins. In the New Testament, every single one of these terms is applied to Jesus!

Jesus said in **John 14:7**, *"If you really know Me, you will know my Father as well."* In **John 10:30** Jesus said, "I and the Father are one." In **John 8:58** Jesus proclaimed He was eternal. In **Matthew 28:18** Jesus affirmed that He was all-powerful, and in **Matthew 28:20** Jesus declared that He was all-present. Jesus: 1) claimed to be God, 2) had the attributes of God and, 3) accepted worship as God.

Who do you say I am?

One day Jesus asked His disciples a question. He said: *"'Who do the crowds say I am?'* (**Luke 9:18**) The disciples answered that the crowds had various opinions as to Jesus' identity. This is true to this day. People still discuss the identity of Jesus. Jesus made the question more personal when he asked his disciples: *"'But what about you? Who do you say I am?'"* (**Matthew 16:15**) Jesus knew that every individual would have to choose whether or not they would believe Jesus' claims.

You also must make this decision. Who do you believe that Jesus is? If you need to, take more time to study the eyewitness, biographical accounts of Jesus' life found in the Bible. As you study Jesus' claims, and the miracles authenticating His claims, you also must come to a conclusion. Peter, one of Jesus' closest disciples, had no doubt as to who Jesus was. In light of all the overwhelming evidence he had witnessed in Jesus' life, *"Simon Peter answered, 'You are the Christ, the Son of the living God.'"* (**Matthew 16:16**)

PERSONAL & RELEVANT

Topic One: Fact or fiction?

Question: Are the Gospel accounts of Jesus historical or mythical? In order to determine this, analyze the following list:

A Truly Historical Document would make mention of:

Place a checkmark beside the statements that are true:

- ❏ **Events** that are verifiable historically or archaeologically.
- ❏ **Places** that are verifiable historically or archaeologically.
- ❏ **People** that are verifiable historically or archaeologically.

Based on the criteria above, do you think the Gospel records of Jesus are historical? *Why or why not?*

_____

_____

Topic Two: Hanging out

Question: What type of people would you expect a high-profile, popular, miracle working, religious leader to spend time with? What type of people did Jesus spend time with? What does that tell you about who Jesus wanted to relate to? *Popular? Rich? Religious?*

_____

_____

Topic Three: Who exactly is Jesus?

Question: Who did Jesus claim to be? Is there evidence in Jesus' life to back up His claim? If so, mention at least 3 examples that support His claim.
Did He claim to be a great moral teacher? A good person? Messiah? God?

_____

_____

WHAT DOES THIS MEAN FOR *YOU*?

1. Jesus' miracles were evidence for you.

"Jesus' life was characterized by supernatural power. These miracles were the evidence given to back up His claims to be the Messiah, the Son of God. Jesus showed absolute power over the spirit world, the physical world, over sickness and even death itself. Jesus' miracles authenticated His message providing evidence for you to trust Him."

2. Jesus reaches out to you.

"Jesus reached out to people across all social, racial, and ethnic barriers. They were not crowds to Jesus; each person had a face and each face had a name and His offer of life was the same to all. Jesus' offer of life is the same today. He is reaching out to you.

3. You must consider Jesus' claims.

"Jesus claimed to be the Messiah and to be the divine Son of God. These claims were never met with neutral reactions. Jesus confronted people with what they believed. He knew each person would have to choose whether or not to believe His claims. As you study the eye witness accounts, you too must consider Jesus's claims and choose whether to believe them or reject them."

Read it for yourself:

Luke 4:16-21	Jesus announces He is the fulfillment of their prophecies, their Messiah.
John 10:24,25	Jesus says His miracles are the evidence for the fact He is the Messiah the Son of God.
Mark 1:25-27	Jesus casts the demon out of the man.
Matthew 15:30,31	Jesus heals all the sick.
Luke 7:12-16	Jesus raises the dead.
Matthew 14:23	The disciples worship Jesus as God.
Matthew 16:15,16	Who do you say I am?

Dig Deeper

These are not cleverly invented stories, but eyewitness accounts.	**II Peter 1:16-21**
Is there Proof Jesus existed? (Biblical and Extra-Biblical)	**Pg. 151**
Historical Proof outside of the Bible for Jesus' Existence.	**Pg. 153**

Memorize this:

"Jesus answered, 'I am the way, the truth and the life. No one comes to the Father except through Me."
John 14:6

CHAPTER 9

SALVATION

In a heart-to-heart conversation about eternal life, Jesus shows the inadequacy of human efforts. The danger of rejecting the life He offers is a sobering reality seen in the story of one who choses eternal death.

The Words of Eternal Life:

People came to Jesus not only because of what He did, but also because of what He *said*. People were attracted to Him not only because of His power to heal, but also because of His promises to *save*. Jesus had come to save them from eternal punishment. Jesus had come as the Messiah in order to save all of humanity from sin and death. Jesus always spoke the truth courageously and lovingly. Because of this, some people rejected Him; while others, like His disciples, told Him, "…'*You have the words of eternal life.*'"(**John 6:68**)

The Kingdom of God is Near:

Jesus was their long-awaited King, the Messiah, and His kingdom would never end. (**Mark 1:14-15**) To be a part of the kingdom of God, was to be able to live forever, to have eternal life. Jesus further explained that in order to be a part of His kingdom and have this eternal life, two things were needed. Jesus said: "…*[R]epent and believe the good news!*" (**Mark 1:15**)

The Need to Repent:

Repent means to change your mind. You see, the people thought that they were good enough to be accepted by God because of their good works and religious ceremonies. The Pharisees were a religious group of men who devotedly sought after eternal life, but they had wrongly put their confidence in *themselves*. They thought that because of their good works, their ancestry, and all their religious rituals, that they would be guaranteed eternal life. Jesus wanted all people, whether or not they were Pharisees, to realize their works were inadequate and that they were sinners who needed a Savior.

You Must be Born Again:

Nicodemus, himself a Pharisee, was one such man who began to realize that Jesus had come to be their Savior. (**John 3:1**) *"He came to Jesus at night…"* (**John 3:2**) During their conversation, Jesus told Nicodemus, he could not earn eternal life by anything he did. (**John 3:3**) There was only one way to enter the Kingdom of Heaven, being born again. Nicodemus must have been shocked! According to Jesus, all of Nicodemus' plans for earning eternal life and entering into God's kingdom were worthless.

New Spiritual Life:

"Jesus answered, 'I tell you the truth, no one can enter the kingdom of God unless he is born of water and the Spirit.'" (**John 3:4-5**) When Jesus used the phrase "born of water," He was referring to physical birth. Jesus was telling Nicodemus that his physical birth was not enough; Nicodemus needed another birth, one that came from the Spirit of God. Jesus further explained in **John 3:6** that you receive physical life from a physical person, but only the Spirit of God can birth in you spiritual life. No amount of good works, religious ceremonies or following rules can produce this life of God within a person. Only the Spirit of God can give someone this new Life.

Just as Moses Lifted up the Snake:

"How can this be?" Nicodemus asked. (**John 3:9**) In order to answer Nicodemus' question, Jesus referred to an event that had taken place in Israel's history during their desert travels. When the people had rebelled against Him, God sent venomous snakes among them. But when the people cried out for deliverance, God told Moses to make a snake and place it on a pole. Whenever anyone looked at the snake, God gave them life. (**Numbers 21:4-9**) Jesus told Nicodemus, *"Just as Moses lifted up the snake in the desert, so the Son of Man must be lifted up, that everyone who believes in Him may have eternal life."* (**John 3:14-15**)

Sin Condemns us to Death:

Just as the snakebite caused the people to die, so too, the sin within us condemns us to death, for the payment for sin is death. No amount of good works or religious ceremonies can reverse the effects of our fatal condition. In the desert, God did not force His healing upon anyone. In the same way, Jesus did not force anyone to accept His offer of life. Each person would have to choose whether or not they would believe in Him. Jesus explained to Nicodemus, *"For God so loved the world that He gave His one and only Son, that whoever believes in Him shall not perish but have eternal life."* (**John 3:16**)

Just Believe:

Believe? Was Jesus really telling Nicodemus to just believe? Was that all that was required of him in order to gain entrance into Heaven? It seemed too easy. Surely God demanded more.

What does God require for entrance into Heaven? How would you answer if someone asked you, "What must I do to get to Heaven?" Be a good citizen? Help the poor? Do good works? Pray? Fast? Take part in religious ceremonies or even pilgrimages? What does God require?

When Jesus was asked to give a list of the works that God required, read how He answered in **John 6:29**. Jesus said the only thing that God asks you and me to do is to *believe* in the One God has sent: Jesus.

You can be Declared Righteous:

(**John 3:17**) Jesus came to save, not to condemn people; their sins already condemned them! God wants to offer us forgiveness and make us completely acceptable to Him. When God declares someone righteous that means their sins are completely forgiven, and they are fully acceptable to God. All who believe in Jesus as the Messiah and Christ will be declared righteous. (**Romans 3:22**) Jesus explained to Nicodemus that, *"Whoever believes in Him is not condemned, but whoever does not believe stands condemned already because he has not believed in the name of God's one and only Son."* (**John 3:18**)

One Way to Eternal Life:

Believe or reject Jesus. Receive eternal life or continue in a condition of being eternally condemned for your sins. This was the choice that God was offering. In **John 8:24** Jesus earnestly warned the people that if they didn't believe He was who He claimed to be, the Messiah who had come to save them, then they would eternally die because of their sins. There was only one way to be saved. In **Genesis 6-8**, because of all the wickedness and violence that had filled the earth, God sent a global flood. Just as the ark had been the only way to escape the flood, God has sent Jesus as the only way to escape being judged for our sins. All who refuse to come to Jesus to be saved are rejecting life.

To Reject Life is to Choose Death:

To reject life is to choose death. Jesus was offering *eternal* life. If you reject eternal life, you are choosing eternal death. In **Luke 16**, Jesus described the horrors of eternal death. In this chapter, he told of two men and their final destinies. One of them was a poor, sick and lonely beggar named Lazarus. The other was the rich man at whose gate Lazarus lay. Rich and poor alike, all people are faced with the decision of where they will spend their eternity. Lazarus and the rich man were both sinners, yet Lazarus had repented and chosen to believe God's Word. The rich man, however, had not.

Heaven or Hell:

Luke 16 says the time came when both of these men died. In the same way, that time will come for each one of us. Whether rich or poor, young or old, the time will come for every person on earth to die. And **Hebrews 9:27** says, "...[M]an is destined to die once, and after that to face judgment..." Each person is only given one life. Once that life is over, that person will go to spend eternity in either Heaven or Hell.

According to the Bible, these two places are not allegorical or imaginary. Rather, they are two very real and distinct locations. Heaven is a place of comfort and joy in the presence of God, but Hell is a place of torment and agony, separated from God forever. Lazarus died and was taken to Heaven with Abraham. (**Luke 16:22**) Like Lazarus, when Abraham had been alive on earth, he had believed in God and was declared righteous, completely forgiven, and fully accepted by God. (**Luke 16:22-23**)

The rich man did not go to Hell because he was rich, just as Lazarus did not go to Heaven because he was poor. Actually **Genesis 13** tells us that Abraham was an extremely wealthy man.... and he went to heaven! You see, things like fame, power and money do not follow you or effect you after you die. The reason the rich man went to Hell was because he had not repented; he had not believed in God's Word. During his lifetime he had rejected and ignored God.

Eternal Destinies are Sealed at Death:

In agony he cried out: *"Father Abraham, have pity on me and send Lazarus to dip the tip of his finger in water and cool my tongue, because I am in agony in this fire."* (**Luke 16:24**) Throughout the Scriptures God has made it clear that once a person dies, his eternal destiny is sealed. (**Luke 16:26**) Life with God is forever and those who have chosen God will live with Him for all of eternity. Those who have chosen to reject God, however, will be separated from Him forever. Eternal life is as permanent as eternal death. Those who are in Hell can never leave.

God's Word Convinces us to Believe:

The rich man could not bear the thought of his brothers also coming to Hell. (**Luke 16:27-28**) He begged Lazarus to go back to earth and warn them. He hoped that this would convince them to repent and believe God's Word.[7] Abraham knew that if the brothers had rejected God's Word, not even someone coming back from the dead would convince them. (**Luke 16:31**) You see, it is God's Word that convinces us to believe the truth. While the brothers were still alive, they had an opportunity to listen to God's Word and believe. You and I

---

[7] Moses and the Prophets: Another way of describing God's Word.

also have this opportunity, to hear the Word of God and put our trust in what He says while we are still alive, and before it is too late.

The Final Passover:

After three years of healing and teaching, Jesus began to head towards Jerusalem. Peter and John were to prepare for the Passover celebration. (**Luke 22:8**) Each year, the Jews went to Jerusalem in order to celebrate the Passover, the time when God had delivered them from slavery in Egypt. Among other observances of the day, one of the most important things they did was to sacrifice a lamb that was then roasted and served at the meal. During the meal, they recalled how God told His people that at midnight the angel of death was to go throughout the land and strike down the firstborn son of every household. On that night, it had not mattered whether a person was good or bad, rich or poor; there was only one thing that determined whether the firstborn son lived or died. God had told them, "[W]hen I see the blood, I will pass over you." (**Exodus 12:13**)

A Greater Deliverance was at Hand:

As they gathered to celebrate the first Passover, the disciples did not realize that an even greater deliverance was at hand. As Jesus took some bread and broke it, He told his disciples that this was the way in which His body would be broken for them. (**Luke 22:19**)

"In the same way, after the supper He took the cup, saying, 'This cup is the new covenant in my blood, which is poured out for you.'" (**Luke 22:20**) At that first Passover long ago, it had been the blood of the lamb that had been shed so that the firstborn son might live. Now Jesus was telling them that *His* own blood was going to be poured out for them, as their Lamb, as their substitute, in order to give them eternal life.

You see, that first Passover had been a picture illustrating and pointing to the death of Jesus Christ. The greatest deliverance was about to take place, one in which men, women and children from all nationalities would be delivered from their bondage to sin and rescued from the punishment of eternal death. Jesus had come in order to pay the ultimate price for our *Salvation*.

PERSONAL & RELEVANT

Topic One: What does God require?

Question: If you were to conduct a survey asking random people in a crowd, "What are the works that God requires for entrance into Heaven?" What are the different responses that people might give?

_____

_____

Questions: What answer did *Jesus* give to this same question? Which answer is correct? *See **John 6:28,29**

_____

_____

Topic Two: "Just as Moses lifted up the snake in the desert..."

Question: In His conversation with Nicodemus as Jesus described the life He came to offer, He referred to an event in Israel's history. *"Just as Moses lifted us the snake in the wilderness, so the Son of Man must be lifted up, that everyone who believes may have eternal life in Him."* (**John 3:14,15**) What do you think Jesus was trying to get across to Nicodemus?

_____

_____

Topic Three: Passover Lamb

Question: Earlier we saw John the Baptist identify Jesus as the Lamb of God. Now during the Passover feast, when the lambs were sacrificed, Jesus talked about His own body being broken; with His own blood being poured out for the forgiveness of sins. What similarities do you see between Jesus and the lamb sacrificed at Passover?

_____

_____

CHAPTER 9: SALVATION

WHAT DOES THIS MEAN FOR *YOU?*

1. You cannot earn eternal life.

"Jesus told the people that in order to have eternal life they needed to repent, or change their minds. The people had wrongly thought they would be accepted by God because of their good works, but Jesus explained that there was only one way to have eternal life: being born again. The Spirit of God is the only One who can give someone this new life. No amount of rules, religious ceremonies, fasts or pilgrimages are enough. You need to repent, change your mind by realizing that no matter how good you are, you cannot earn eternal life. Like Nicodemus, you also need this new spiritual life that only God can give you."

2. The only thing you must do is believe in Jesus Christ.

"Jesus told Nicodemus that whoever believed in Him would have eternal life. Jesus explained that just as Moses lifted up the snake in the desert, He too would be lifted up. In the desert, those who were dying from the snakebite had only to believe what God said and look and they would have life. You are like those who were dying in the desert because your sin condemns you to death. In order to be saved, the only thing that God requires is for you to believe in His Son, Jesus Christ, and you will have eternal life."

3. God wants you to go to Heaven.

"God has planned eternal life to be in a real and wonderful place of comfort and joy called Heaven. All those who believe in Jesus Christ will enjoy the presence of God forever. But, all who refuse to come to Jesus to be saved are rejecting eternal life and choosing eternal death. Eternal death is separation from God forever in a real place of torment and agony called Hell. God wants you to go to Heaven. He desires you to be saved and not perish."

4. Jesus came to be your Passover Lamb.

"Jesus and his disciples gathered to celebrate the passover. At the first passover long ago in Egypt, it had been the blood of the lamb that had been shed so that the firstborn son might live. But now, Jesus was explaining that His body would be broken for you. And that His own blood was going to be poured out. Jesus came to be your Passover Lamb, to be your substitute, so that you could have eternal life."

Read it for yourself:

Mark 1:14,15	Jesus tells the people to repent and believe.
John 3:1-18	Jesus tells Nicodemus how to have eternal life.
John 6:28,29	What are the works God requires?
Luke 16:19-31	Lazarus and the rich man die.
Luke 22:19,20	Jesus celebrates the Passover.

Dig Deeper

Jesus says He is the way, the truth, and the life	**John 14:6**
God does not want anyone to perish.	**II Peter 3:9**
How could a loving God send people to Hell?	**Pg. 156**
Life now, life then, life after death?	**Pg. 158**

Memorize this:

"*For God so loved the world that He gave His one and only Son, that whoever believes in Him shall not perish but have eternal life.*" **John 3:16**

CHAPTER 10

IT IS FINISHED

Jesus is the final sacrifice. On the cross, He shouts, "Tetelestai!" proclaiming our enemies defeat, the restoration of our broken relationship with God, and hope for all humanity.

Eternal Plan of Salvation:

During the Passover meal, only Jesus fully understood what was going to happen as Judas, one of his twelve disciples, set into motion a series of events that had been part of God's plan from before time began. In the very first book of the Bible, in **Genesis 3:15**, God gave the very first promise concerning the Messiah. By saying that the Messiah's heel would be bruised, God foretold the fact that in the process of completely defeating Satan, that the Messiah Himself would suffer.

For the next thousands of years, God further described His Plan of Salvation, in countless, specific prophecies woven throughout the scriptures. King David foretold the Messiah's betrayal, mocking, crucifixion, the soldiers who would gamble for his clothing, and even some of the Messiah's last words. (**Psalm 22**) Daniel foretold the exact time that the Messiah would die. (**Daniel 9:25-26**) Isaiah wrote that the Messiah would be beaten, flogged, and led like a lamb to the slaughter. (**Isaiah 53**) And Zechariah wrote that they would look on the One they had pierced. (**Zechariah 12:10**) Every single one of these prophecies, and more, were about to be fulfilled by Jesus Christ.

The Time was Drawing Near:

After Jesus and His disciples celebrated the Passover feast together, they left Jerusalem and went to a garden where Jesus had frequently gone to pray. There, Jesus was experiencing deep sorrow because He knew that the time was drawing near in which He would die. (**Mark 14:34**) Now, this didn't take Jesus by surprise. In fact, on three separate occasions, Jesus had already patiently explained to his disciples everything that He was about to go through. (**Mark 10:33-34**) Jesus knew that He was about to face more than excruciating pain and death. Jesus was about to take all of the punishment for our sins upon Himself, and be cursed by God. This is what Jesus dreaded more than the physical pain and death that He was about to endure.

No Other Way:

Three times that night Jesus prayed, begging His Father that if there be any other way to resolve the problem of sin and rescue humanity – that He be spared from what He was about to endure. (**Mark 14:36**) But there was no other way. No religious system, no amount of good works, no pilgrimage, no ritual, no ceremony would ever be adequate. For all had sinned, and the payment for sin is death. Jesus knew that in order to rescue humanity, He would have to die.

Fulfilling God's Rescue Plan:

Judas, one of Jesus' twelve disciples, had been paid off by the religious leaders to betray Jesus and hand him over to them. (**Mark 14:43-46**) As they arrested Jesus, He proclaimed that everything that was happening, was happening in order to fulfill the Scriptures, the Word of God. (**Mark 14:48-49**) For Jesus was not leading a rebellion, but a rescue; a rescue planned before the creation of the world and foretold in the Scriptures.

Condemned as Worthy of Death:

After Jesus' arrest, His enemies proceeded to hold an illegal trial in the middle of the night. (**Mark 14:55-56**) Wanting to justify their hatred of Jesus, they procured false witnesses. Finally, "*[T]he high priest asked Him, 'Are you the Christ, the Son of the Blessed One?' 'I am,' said Jesus.*" (**Mark 14:61-62**) When Jesus claimed to be their Messiah, the Son of God, the chief priest responded, "'*You have heard the blasphemy. What do you think?' They all condemned Him as worthy of death.*" (**Mark 14:64**)

The Guilty One Set Free:

After separately questioning Jesus, both Herod and Pontius Pilate came to the same conclusion: Jesus was innocent. "*Now it was the governor's custom at the Feast to release a prisoner chosen by the crowd. At that time they had a notorious prisoner called Barabbas…*" (**Matthew 27:15-16**) Barabbas was in prison with the insurrectionists who had committed murder in a recent uprising. (**Matthew 27:17-26**) Finally, after trying in vain to reason with the multitude of Jesus' innocence, Pontius Pilate, "*…released Barabbas to them. But he had Jesus flogged, and handed him over to be crucified.*" (**Matthew 27:26**)

Barabbas was a murderer and a law-breaker, Jesus was the perfect Son of God. On that day, however, it was the guilty one who was released. The guilty one was set free and given life because an innocent One was condemned and sentenced to death. You see, as the prisoner set free, Barabbas unknowingly represented you and me. We have broken God's holy laws; we are guilty and condemned. Yet Jesus came in order to take our condemnation, that we might be set free. Jesus came to die so that we might live.

His Body was Broken:

Before Jesus was crucified, Pilate had him flogged. Flogging was extremely brutal. A whip was made from braided leather and contained metal balls that would strike the victim, causing deep contusions. Pieces of bone that had been woven into the leather, shredded the victim's flesh. Many people died just from the floggings. After the soldiers had also mocked and beat Jesus, they led Him out to be crucified. (**Mark 15:17-20**)

Jesus' Love Held Him There:

At nine o'clock in the morning, they stretched out the hands of a trembling Jewish carpenter. These were the hands that had healed lepers. These hands had reached out to sinners and outcasts, but now they were being pierced. Why? Couldn't Jesus have stopped them? Weren't these the hands of the One who had commanded death and demons? Weren't these the feet of the One who had walked on water? Yes, they were. Jesus could have stopped them, but He chose not to. Though they nailed him to a cross, His love for you and me would have held Him there. As the pain from nail-smashed nerves, the dizziness from blood loss, and the throbbing of dislocated joints ravaged His body, *"Jesus said, "Father, forgive them, for they do not know what they are doing."* (**Luke 23:34**)

The Worst of All Agonies:

"At the sixth hour darkness came over the whole land until the ninth hour." (**Mark 15:33**) Darkness covered the land for three hours, from noon, until three o'clock in the afternoon. After Jesus had been hanging on the cross for six hours, He faced the most indescribable pain of all. In incredible anguish, Jesus cried out, *"My God, my God, why have you forsaken me?"* (**Mark 15:34**) This spiritual separation was the worst of all agonies.
2 Corinthians 5:21 says, Jesus, who had no sin, took our sins upon Himself. God took the punishment for all of those sins, and poured it out upon His Son, Jesus. (**Isaiah 53:6**) **Isaiah 53:5** says, *"[H]e was crushed for our iniquities; the punishment that brought us peace was upon Him."*

Rejected so We Could be Accepted:

Note also that Jesus said "My God, my God" and not, "My Father, my Father". On the cross, Jesus was taking our place, and enduring the wrath of God in order to give guilty sinners like you and me the right to do the unthinkable: the right to call all-Holy God, "Father."

Tetelestai: It is Finished:

Then, knowing that all was now completed, Jesus cried out: "...'It is finished.'" (**John 19:30**) Just before Jesus died, He proclaimed one of the most important phrases in all of history, "It is finished." This phrase comes from the Greek word *tetelestai*. *Tetelestai* was also a word that meant fulfilled, carried out, and completed. Jesus had fulfilled the prophecies. He had carried out all the requirements of God's perfect Laws. Jesus had completed what God had commanded Him to do. It was finished!

Tetelestai: Paid in Full:

Tetelestai also meant "paid in full". In this sense, it was used as a legal term. When a debt had been fully met, it was declared "Tetelestai", paid in full. You see, you and I also have a debt that we need to pay. We are sinners, and God has declared that, "the payment for sin is death." (**Romans 6:23**) Jesus had come in order to pay our debt for us. Jesus fully paid for our sins. There is no more payment, there is no more punishment or sacrifice left for me or you to offer God for the forgiveness of our sins. It is finished, it is Tetelestai!

Complete Access to all-Holy God:

When Jesus shouted "Tetelestai" something extraordinary happened within the temple. Now remember, like the tabernacle, within the Temple a thick curtain blocked the access into the Most Holy Place. But when Jesus shouted "Tetelestai" – It is finished, "...*the curtain of the temple was torn in two from top to bottom.*" (**Matthew 27:51**) The blood of Jesus Christ, the Lamb of God, had been poured out for the sins of the world! Jesus was the final sacrifice. In this way, atonement was made not temporarily, but once and for all! God's punishment was turned away from us. The curtain that separated man from God was torn from top to bottom to show that now, because of the sacrifice of Jesus, guilty sinners like you and me could have complete access to the all-Holy God!

Jesus Was Dead:

To get the bodies off the crosses before the Sabbath, the soldiers had been ordered to break the legs of all those who were crucified. John, a disciple of Jesus, was there at the foot of the cross. **John 19:33-34** tell us that when Jesus' side was pierced, it brought forth blood and water. When Jesus died a collection of fluids built up in the membranes surrounding Jesus' lungs and heart. The soldier's spear most likely pierced Jesus' right side, puncturing those membranes, causing the flow of blood and water. Medical doctor, Alexander Metherell, states that, "There was absolutely no doubt that Jesus was dead."

An Empty Tomb:

After Jesus died, Joseph, a follower of Jesus, along with Nicodemus, obtained permission from Pilate to take His body. **Mark 15:46-47** says that they placed Jesus' body in a tomb cut out of rock. Yet, **Luke 24:1-6** records, *"On the first day of the week, very early in the morning, the women took the spices they had prepared and went to the tomb. They found the stone rolled away from the tomb, but when they entered, they did not find the body of the Lord Jesus. While they were wondering about this, suddenly two men in clothes that gleamed like lightning stood beside them. But the men said to them, "Why do you look for the living among the dead? He is not here; he has risen!"*

A Resurrected Messiah:

Romans 1:4 says that Jesus' resurrection proved that He was the son of God, the Messiah. Jesus' resurrection was also proof that He had defeated death. In **John 11:25**, Jesus claimed, *"…I am the resurrection and the life. He who believes in me will live, even though He dies…"* Through Jesus' resurrection, He could now offer what every human being longs for, the guarantee of eternal life even after death. Finally, Jesus' resurrection was the evidence that God had accepted the sacrifice of the innocent Lamb of God. It is finished: Tetelestai!

PERSONAL & RELEVANT

Topic One: Barabbas and you

Question: If we were to compare ourselves to Barabbas, what do we have in common with him?

_____

_____

Topic Two: It is finished

Question: If someone asked, "What are the worst things you have ever done?", it would be too humiliating to list. Instead, list below the sins that plague humanity in general. *Pornography, drugs, hate…*

_____

Question: Read **Isaiah 53:5**. At the moment of the crucifixion, what did God do with your sins? *Your sins and the sins of the entire world.* When you think about what He did, what are your thoughts and feelings?

Hint: Transgressions and iniquities are words that mean "sin."

_____

Question: Why did Jesus say, "It is Finished"? How does that phrase impact your life?

_____

_____

Topic Three: Access to God

Question: Why was there a Curtain separating people from entering into the Most Holy Place? *What did the Curtain remind the people of?*

_____

Question: Why was the Curtain torn from top to bottom when Jesus died on the cross?

_____

WHAT DOES THIS MEAN FOR *YOU*?

1. Barabbas is a picture of you.

"Barabbas was guilty and deserved to be condemned. Yet Jesus was innocent, and deserved to be set free. On that day however, Barabbas was released, but Jesus was flogged and handed over to be crucified. You see, Barabbas is a picture of you. You also are guilty before God and deserve to be punished. Yet God gave His innocent Son to be condemned, so that you could be set free."

2. Jesus completely paid for your sins.

"The payment for sin is death. On the cross, God laid each one of your sins upon Jesus. God punished Him by pouring out His wrath on Jesus. Right before Jesus died, he shouted: "Tetelestai". Which means, 'It is Finished!' He was proclaiming that He had done everything necessary to pay for your sins. That means there is nothing left for you to do. There are no more sacrifices you must offer. There are no good works to fulfill. Jesus has completely paid for your sins."

3. You can have access to God.

"In the temple there was a thick curtain that blocked the access into the Most Holy Place. Only once a year did one man go behind the curtain into God's presence. But when Jesus shouted, "Tetelestai: it is finished"; the curtain that separated mankind from God was torn from top to bottom to show that because of Jesus' sacrifice, now you can have access to God."

4. Jesus offers eternal life to you.

"During Jesus' ministry, some of His critics had demanded He give them a miraculous sign to prove His authority. Jesus had told them that the final sign that would prove who He was would be this; when they had killed Him three days later He would rise from the dead. Jesus' resurrection is the proof that He is who He claimed to be; the Son of God, the Messiah. Jesus' resurrection demonstrates that His words can be trusted, and that He can truly offer eternal life to you."

CHAPTER 10: IT IS FINISHED

Read it for yourself:

Mark 10:33,34	Jesus explains to his disciples how He will be betrayed, killed, and raise to life.
Mark 14:32-64	Jesus is betrayed and tried by the religious leaders.
Matthew 27:15-26	Jesus is condemned; Barabbas is released.
Mark 15:17-20	Jesus is flogged and mocked.
Luke 23:34	Jesus prays, "Father forgive them…"
John 19:30	Jesus proclaims, "It is finished!"
Matthew 27:51	The Curtain in the temple is torn.
John 19:33,34	Jesus' heart is pierced.
Mark 14:46,47	Jesus is buried in the tomb.
Luke 24:1-6	The women find the empty tomb.

Dig Deeper

Jesus died for our sins once and for all.	**I Peter 3:18**
Jesus had no sins and yet was punished in our place.	**II Corinthians 5:21**
Why did Jesus have to die?	**Pg. 162**
Why should I believe in the resurrection?	**Pg. 166**
Beyond Blind Faith	**Pg. 171**

Memorize this:

"For the wages of sin is death, but the gift of God is Eternal Life in Christ Jesus our Lord." **Romans 6:23**

CHAPTER 11

ETERNAL LIFE

An empty tomb, startled eye witnesses and the unexpected visit of the risen Jesus lead to a life changing journey through the Scriptures that reveals the Eternal Story of Redemption; a story that could change you forever

---

God's Eternal Plan of Salvation:

The disciples were both amazed and overwhelmed. (**Luke 24:36-39**) They had so many questions. They were certain Jesus was their Messiah who would reign forever. But they couldn't understand why He had allowed Himself to be crucified. Jesus explained to His disciples how His death and resurrection were God's Plan to rescue humanity, defeat Satan, and restore their broken relationship with God. As Jesus explained the Scriptures to them, they realized that from the very beginning, God had been writing His Eternal Story. (**Luke 24:44-45**) As we go over some of these Scriptures together, I hope that you also will understand and believe God's Plan of Salvation.

You were Created for a Relationship with God:

God, who is eternal, all-powerful, all-knowing, and all-present, created the heavens and the earth. In this perfect world, God created the first man and woman in His image, so that they might have a relationship with Him. You and I were also created for a relationship with God, created to enjoy His love. God, however, does not force us to love and obey Him, for real love is only love if it is a choice. God told Adam and Eve not to eat fruit from the Tree of the Knowledge of Good and Evil, or they would surely die. If they were to reject God, they would be choosing death.

Sin Brings Separation Between You and God:

Satan, an angel who had rebelled against God, came to the Garden as a snake in order to deceive Adam and Eve into doubting God's Word and His love. Adam and Eve chose to listen to Satan's lies, and disobeyed God. At that moment, sin entered the world. Sin is anything that goes against the perfect character of God. God is holy, which means He is completely pure, with nothing evil in Him. Adam and Eve's sin brought separation between them and God.

The Deliverer would Restore the Broken Relationship:
Driven by their shame, guilt, and fear, Adam and Eve tried in vain to resolve the problem of their sin in their own strength. Just as Adam and Eve's leaf clothes did not take away their shame and guilt, you and I cannot resolve the problem of our sin. God in His love, promised them that one day a Deliverer would be born without a human father. This Son would crush Satan's power over them, restoring the broken relationship between God and humanity.

You were Born a Sinner:
Adam and Eve had to leave the Garden. Adam's sin was passed down to each one of his descendants. You and I are born sinners, separated from God. The sin within the heart of every person is the cause for all of the suffering and evil in the world today.

God Desires a Relationship with You:
But God's desire was still for a relationship with humanity. Those who wanted this relationship, like Noah and his family, were still sinners but because they believed God they were made righteous. Their sins were forgiven by God. Tragically though, the rest of the world wanted nothing of God's forgiveness. As people rejected God, they became increasingly evil and corrupt.

The Ark - Pictured the One Way to be Saved through Jesus:
Because God is holy and must punish sin, a judgment of flood waters would be sent upon the earth. In His mercy, God provided one way to be saved; this was a picture of the salvation God offers only through Jesus. In the same way, our sins deserve judgment. If we reject Jesus, we are just like those who refused to enter the ark and died in the Flood. By rejecting Jesus you are rejecting the only way to be saved. Just as those who entered the ark lived, God in His love provided Jesus as the only way for you and me to live and escape His judgment.

The Deliverer would be a Descendant of Abraham:
After the Flood, Noah's descendants spread out over the earth. It was during the lifetime of Noah's son, Shem, that Abraham was born. God told Abraham that He was leading him to a land that would be his possession. God promised Abraham that His family would become a great nation through whom all people on earth would be blessed; for the Deliverer would come from this nation. Even though he and his wife Sarah were elderly and

barren, Abraham put his faith in what God said. Because of Abraham's faith, God declared Abraham to be righteous, with all his sins forgiven.

Like the Ram - God Provided Jesus as a Substitute for You:

God gave Abraham and Sarah their son, Isaac. In a divine test, God asked Abraham to offer Isaac as a sacrifice to Him. God had promised that a nation, and the Deliverer, would come through Isaac. Although Abraham did not understand, he obeyed. As they journeyed up the mountain, Abraham told Isaac that God Himself would provide a lamb for the sacrifice. Because of our sin, you and I are also condemned to death. But God Himself intervened. Just as God provided a ram to be killed in Isaac's place, God provided Jesus as a substitute for you and me. Jesus died in the place of a world condemned to death.

Like the Passover Lamb - Jesus is Our Perfect Lamb

Isaac had a son named Jacob, whose name was changed to Israel. Israel's twelve sons formed the nation through which the Deliverer would come. During a famine, Israel's family went to live in Egypt. Many years later, the Israelites were enslaved.

 In a remarkable series of events, God chose Moses to lead His people. The time had come for God to free the Israelites from their oppression. When God sent ten plagues upon Egypt, He displayed His power as the one true God who would rescue His people from slavery. He was also displaying a picture of the way He would powerfully rescue you and me from slavery to sin and death. You see, during the tenth plague there was only one way for the firstborn son to to escape certain death: a perfect lamb, without blemish, had to be killed in the place of the son, and its blood sprinkled on the doorposts of the home. Jesus was our perfect Lamb. His shed blood is the only way for you and me to escape eternal death.

Jesus can set You Free from Bondage to Sin and Death:

When God miraculously freed the slaves from the hand of their oppressors and brought them to safety, it was a picture of what God wants to do for you and me. We can be set free from our bondage to sin and death through the blood of Jesus shed for you and me on the cross.

The Law Reveals We Need Jesus to Rescue Us:

Before bringing the Israelites into the land He had promised to their ancestor Abraham, God led them to Mt. Sinai. There, God gave them the Ten Commandments. Because God is Holy, completely pure, with nothing evil in Him, God requires perfect obedience to His laws. God's standards go far beyond mere outward conformity. His standards deal with our words and even our deepest thoughts. The people, however, were sinners and disobeyed God's laws over and over again. We also, are like the Israelites; we too, have disobeyed God's commandments. Just as a mirror reveals imperfections, God's laws reveal the sinfulness of our hearts. They help us realize how much we need Jesus to rescue us from our sins, and restore our broken relationship with God.

Jesus' Blood Turns God's Punishment Away from You:

The Ten Commandments were placed in a golden box called the Ark of the Covenant, which was located in the Most Holy Place of the Tabernacle. Access into the Most Holy Place was blocked by an immense, richly ornamented curtain. This was to show that because God is holy, our sin separates us from Him. Only once a year did God allow the High Priest behind the curtain and into His presence, but never without the blood of the sacrifice. Inside the Ark of the Covenant were God's holy laws that show our complete sinfulness, and how much we deserve condemnation and death. Above the Atonement cover, was the presence of God. When God looked down, instead of seeing the laws that condemn, He chose to see the blood of the innocent one. In the same way, the laws that condemn you and me are covered by the blood of Jesus, in order to turn God's punishment away from us.

Jesus was Lifted Up to Give You Eternal Life:

Years later when the Israelites rebelled against God in the desert, a judgment of venomous snakes was sent upon the people. It was impossible for anyone bitten to produce a remedy to reverse the poison; the bite was fatal. God in His mercy, however, provided a way for all those who were bitten to be healed. All they had to do was believe what God said, look at the bronze snake, and they would be given life. Just as Moses lifted up the bronze snake in the desert, Jesus was lifted up, so that all who put their faith in Him will not perish but be given eternal life.

Messiah - Title for the Deliverer:

Those who eagerly awaited the arrival of the Deliverer began to refer to Him as the "Anointed One" or the "Messiah". Throughout Israel's history, God gave His people numerous prophecies describing who the Messiah would be, and what the Messiah would do.

Jesus Did Not have a Human Father:

Hundreds of years after these prophecies were given, God sent the angel Gabriel to announce to a virgin that she would give birth to the Messiah who would be called Jesus. Just as God had promised to Adam and Eve, the Messiah would not have a human father, for He would be the *'Son of God'*. This good news of great joy was for all people. The Son of God, the One who had spoken the stars into existence, had taken on human form. Just as it had been prophesied, *"The virgin will conceive and give birth to a Son and they will call Him Immanuel, which means God with us."* (**Matthew 1:22**)

Jesus Perfectly Obeyed God's Laws:

When Jesus was about thirty years old, God sent John the Baptist to prepare the people's hearts for the Messiah. John told the people that they needed to repent, to change their minds, and admit they were sinners who needed a Savior. At Jesus' baptism God announced that His Son, Jesus, was the One who pleased Him. Jesus was the only One who perfectly obeyed God's laws and did not sin.

Jesus Came to be Examined in Your Place:

Jesus demonstrated this when He had total victory over Satan's temptations. Jesus lived the perfect sinless life that you and I cannot live, in order to be our perfect substitute. Just as the lambs for the sacrifice were examined instead of the sinner, Jesus came to be examined in our place. He came to be, *"The Lamb of God who takes away the sins of the world!"* (**John 1:29**)

Jesus is the Promised Messiah:

After His baptism, Jesus openly proclaimed that He was the Messiah they had been waiting for. To back up this claim, Jesus demonstrated supernatural power and authority over the spirit world as He fulfilled the prophecies that said the Messiah would proclaim freedom for the prisoners and release the oppressed. Jesus also"...*healed all the sick. This was to fulfill what was spoken through the prophet Isaiah: 'He took up our infirmities and carried our diseases."* (**Matthew 8:16-17**) Jesus had power over death itself. As Jesus reached out to the needy, the hurting and the outcasts, He demonstrated love like nothing the world has ever seen.

Jesus is God:

When his disciples were caught in a terrifying storm, Jesus came to them walking on the water, and brought total peace to the storm. The disciples realized that only God could walk on water. Only God could instantly calm the wind and the waves, and only God is worthy of our worship. In light of all they had seen and heard in Jesus' life, many like Peter, came to the conclusion that Jesus was the Messiah, the Son of God.

You Cannot Save Yourself - Only Jesus Can:

As the Messiah, Jesus spoke of the eternal life that He offered. Jesus told the people they needed to repent, change their minds. The people had wrongly thought they would be accepted by God because of their good works. Like Nicodemus, they needed to realize that their failure to obey all of God's laws condemned them to eternal death. They could not save themselves through their own efforts. This is why Jesus had come.

When Jesus and his disciples gathered to celebrate the Passover, Jesus told them that *His* own blood was going to be poured out. Jesus had come to be the Passover Lamb. His death would be the only way to rescue the world. No religious system, no pilgrimage, or good works the people tried to offer God, would ever be sufficient. For all had sinned, and the payment for sin is death. Jesus had come to make that payment.

Tetelestai - Jesus is the Final Sacrifice:

All of history had been pointing to this moment. The One who could calm a raging sea, allowed Himself to be taken by an angry mob. The Innocent One was tried and condemned, so that the guilty ones could be released and set free. Jesus was crushed for our iniquities. The punishment that brought us peace was upon Him. The Sinless One had lived the life that you and I could not live; then He died the death that we deserve. Just as God had provided a substitute for Isaac; just as the blood of the Passover lamb had been poured out: every single sacrifice had been pointing to this moment. On the cross, Jesus poured out His blood for the sins of the world! The Enemy's power was crushed. Jesus shouted: *Tetelestai*! It is Finished! Jesus was the final sacrifice! Our sins were paid in full. At that moment, the veil in the temple was torn in two; the way to God was opened! The broken relationship between sinful man and Holy God could be restored.

Jesus Offers Eternal Life to all who Believe:

On the third day, Jesus rose again, just as the Scriptures had foretold. The sacrifice of the innocent Lamb of God had been accepted. Jesus had completely conquered death! Through Jesus' resurrection, He now offers eternal life to all who believe.

A Glimpse of Eternal Life:

We are given a glimpse of this eternal life in the book of Revelation. In Heaven, there will be people from every tribe, language, people and nation worshipping Jesus and thanking Him for having died in their place to give them Eternal Life. (**Revelation 5:9**) They will be a part of His Eternal Kingdom where Jesus, the Messiah, will reign forever.

It is No Accident You are Hearing this Message Today:

It is no accident that you are hearing this message today. Do you realize how much God loves you? He created you to have a relationship with Him. This relationship is only possible through Jesus Christ. Jesus said in **John 14:6**: *"I am the way, the truth and the life. No one comes to the Father except through Me."* **Romans 6:23** says, *"For the wages of sin is death, but the gift of God is eternal life in Christ Jesus our Lord."*

Grace - Favor we do not Deserve: Will You Accept it?

You see, because of your sin, what you deserve is death, but Jesus has already come and paid the price for your sins, so that He can give you eternal life. This is what the Bible calls "grace". Grace is "favor that we do not deserve". By providing Jesus as the sacrifice for our sins, God has shown us His grace, His favor that we do not deserve.

In order to receive this grace, God says all we need is faith. Faith is believing that what God says is true. **Ephesians 2:8-9** says, "...*it is by grace you have been saved through faith and this is not from yourselves, it is the gift of God, not by works, so that no one can boast.*" When you believe that what God says is true - that Jesus is the final sacrifice for your sins and that He has risen again - then you will receive eternal life as a gift. It's free. You don't have to pay for it. Jesus has already paid the ultimate price for your rescue. The only thing you need to do is accept it!

What do you believe?

Instructions: Fill this out honestly from your heart. Unlike all of the group discussions in this Bible Study, this isn't time to talk and formulate answers as a group. It's a quiet time to fill out what *you* believe.

This is a chance to examine your own heart in light of all you have studied in God's Word. If you already have a relationship with Jesus, then see this time as a chance to articulate what you believe in preparation to share this hope with others.

Take as much space as you need to fill out your answers.

1. Do you consider yourself to be a sinner? *(Please explain)*

   _____
   _____
   _____

2. What does God say the payment for sin is?

   _____
   _____
   _____

3. If you were having a conversation with someone, and that person told you, *"I don't believe Jesus is God. I think He was only a wise teacher, a good man, and an example to follow."* How would you respond?

   _____
   _____
   _____

4. If God says that the "wages [or payment] for sin is death" but Jesus was not a sinner, then why did He die and rise again?

   _____
   _____
   _____

5. Do you think you're going to Heaven?
   - If I've been good enough and God thinks I deserve it, then I guess I will.
   - No, I think I've sinned too many times.
   - I think so, but many times I'm afraid I'm not going to Heaven.
   - Absolutely yes! I have no doubts!
   - Other:

   _____
   _____
   _____

6. If you were to die today and stand before God and He were to ask you, "Why should I let you into Heaven?" What would you say? *(Please explain)*

   _____
   _____
   _____

7. After finishing this Bible Study:
   - I believe Jesus is the Messiah who died and rose again to pay for my sins.
   - I'm not sure what to believe. I have questions about:

   _____
   _____
   _____

Read it for yourself:

Romans 3:23	Each one of us is a sinner. We cannot measure up to God's standards, we fall short.
John 3:16	God loved us so much that He sent His Son. Whoever believes in Him is not condemned but given eternal life.
Romans 6:23	The payment for sin is death. The gift that God gives us is eternal life through Jesus.
Ephesians 2:8,9	This gift God gives us is by grace which means that it cannot be earned by anything that we do.

Dig Deeper

Jesus died for our sins once and for all.	**I Peter 3:18**
Jesus had no sins and yet was punished in our place.	**II Corinthians 5:21**

Memorize this:

"This is love: not that we loved God, but that He loved us and sent His Son as an atoning sacrifice for our sins." **John 4:10**

CHAPTER 12

WHAT DO YOU BELIEVE?

Whether you are trying to make a decision for yourself or equipping yourself to help others, it is crucial to examine these life-changing questions in light of the Bible.

1. Do you consider yourself to be a sinner?

Read: Romans 3:23

This verse says we are all sinners and that we've fallen short of God's glory, which means we don't reach His standard.

1. *You were born a sinner.*

    Adam's sin was passed down to each of us (**Romans 5:12**) which means every single one of us was already born a sinner (**Psalm 51:5**) The Bible says that anyone who claims they don't have sin is a liar. (**I John 1:8**)

2. *You've broken God's holy laws.*

    God gave us His holy laws (**Exodus 20:1-17**) but because we are sinners, we are incapable of keeping them perfectly. (**James 2:10**) God's laws help us recognize how sinful we are and how much we need the Savior. (**Romans 3:20**)

2. What does God say the payment for sin is?

Read: Romans 6:23a.

The wages, or payment, for sin is death.

1. *After death we will give account to God.*

   Each one of us has one life to live. After death we will stand before God in judgment. (**Hebrews 9:27**) All of our actions, words and thoughts are recorded by God in the books being written about our life. We will be judged by these books. (**Revelation 20:12**)

2. *Separation from God is eternal.*

   If we are not rescued from our sins, then after we die, we will face eternal separation from God in the lake of fire. (**Luke 16:22-31**)

3. If you were having a conversation with someone and that person told you, "I don't believe Jesus is God. I think He was only a wise teacher, a good man, and an example to follow." How would you respond?

Read: John 1:1-3, 14 - Jesus is God. Jesus came down to earth as a human in order to be our Savior.

Read: Philippians 2:6-11 - Even though Jesus was in fact God, He came to the earth to die on the cross for our sins.

1. **Jesus claimed to be God.**

   In **John 10**, the religious leaders told Jesus they were going to kill Him for claiming to be God. If they had been misinterpreting Jesus, then at this time Jesus would have said, "Oh, no, you misunderstood Me! I wasn't claiming to be God!" but Jesus did not say that! They had not misunderstood His actions and words. He was, in fact, stating He was God! (**John 10:30-33**)

   *See also: **John 8:24, 28; 56, 59; 18:5**; - Jesus repeatedly used the term "I Am." (God's name for Himself in **Exodus 3:14**.) **John 14:6-10** - Jesus claims to be the only way to Heaven and also claims to be One with the Father. Jesus describes Himself as the "first and the last" ,(**Revelation 1:17,18**) a term that is used by God in **Isaiah 44:6**. (See also **Revelation 22:13-16**)

2. Jesus had the attributes of God.

Jesus has the titles of God:

In the Old Testament, some of God's titles are: King, Judge, Light, Rock, Redeemer, Creator[8], the Giver of life, the One who speaks with divine authority and the One who has the ability to forgive sins[9]. In the New Testament, every single one of these terms is applied to Jesus!

Jesus has the characteristics of God[10]:

Jesus is Eternal (**John 8:58**) Jesus is All-powerful (**Matthew 28:18**) Jesus is All-present. (**Matthew 28:20**)

Jesus is referred to as God:

The prophecy about the Messiah who would be a Son who was given, a child who was born. This child would be called "Mighty God" (**Isaiah 9:6**) The angel said Jesus would be called "God with us." (**Matthew 1:23**) God the Father refers to His Son Jesus as "God" (**Hebrews 1:8,9**) Jesus is described as the "fullness of Deity in bodily form." (**Colossians 2:9**)

Thomas, Jesus' disciple, upon seeing the risen Jesus and His nail marked hands exclaims, "My Lord and my God!" - Again, if Jesus were not God; He would have said, "Whoah! Wait a second Thomas, I'm not God," but Jesus accepted Thomas's statement and his worship. (**John 20:27-28**)

3. Jesus accepted worship as God.

When Jesus calmed the storm, His disciples worshipped Him proclaiming, "Truly, you are the Son of God!" Worship of anyone other than God is strictly forbidden in the Bible. If Jesus were merely a man, if He were only a good teacher or a prophet, He would have instantly rebuked them for worshipping Him. Jesus did not rebuke them; He accepted their worship of Him as God. (**Matthew 14:32,33**)

In scenes the book of Revelation gives us of Heaven, we see both Jesus and the Father being worshipped and given the same glory and honor. (**Revelation 5:13**)[11]

---

[8] In the Old Testament it says God made the world alone by His power. In the New Testament it says Jesus made the world because He is God and the exact representation of His Being. (Isaiah 44:24;/ Hebrews 1:2,3; John 1:1-3) See also: Isaiah 45:12,18; Colossians 1:15-17

[9] Matthew 9:1-8 - When Jesus claimed to be able to forgive sins, the religious leaders rightly realized that He was claiming to do something only God can do.

[10] For the sake of brevity, only these are mentioned but the list could be much more extensive. (Jesus is Holy. Jesus is sinless. Jesus is perfectly loving and perfectly just. Etc.

[11] Angels do not ever accept worship, because they know that worship is for God alone. *(Rev. 22:8,9)*

4. If the Bible says the "wages [or payment] for sin is death" and Jesus was not a sinner, then why did He die?

Read: Romans 6:23 - The payment was death. We are sinners; we deserved to die. However, Jesus came to die *in our place*.

Read: Isaiah 53:5,6 - Our sins were placed on Jesus; He was punished in our place in order to give us forgiveness.

1. Jesus died as our Substitute.

Just as the lambs were examined before sacrifice to see if they were acceptable, Jesus is our perfect Lamb who came to be our substitute! (**John 1:29**) He lived the perfect life we could not live and then died the death that we deserved.

Just as Jesus was condemned and Barabbas was set free, Jesus took our condemnation so that we might be given life! God allowed the innocent One, or righteous One, to die in the place of the guilty ones, or the unrighteous. (**I Peter 3:18; II Corinthians 5:21**)

For more, see also: **Romans 5:8** - *Jesus died for us while we were sinners.*

2. Jesus died to be the final sacrifice for our atonement.

Jesus came to be the final sacrifice for our sins and took our punishment. (**Romans 3:25**) Atonement is the turning aside of God's punishment. God's punishment was forever turned away from us because of trusting in the blood of Jesus as what paid for my sins rather than trusting in our own efforts.

For more: Jesus death fulfilled the Scriptures. (**I Corinthians 15:3,4; Mark 14:48-49**)
Without the shedding of blood there can be no forgiveness. (**Hebrews 9:22**) *Jesus' blood frees us from our sins.* (**Revelation 1:5b**)

> ## 5. Do you think you're going to Heaven?
> ❏ If I've been good enough and God thinks I deserve it, then I guess I will.

Read: James 2:10 - Even if you've done a "good job" keeping God's commands, breaking even *one* of His commands condemns you! God is Holy, which means He is completely pure with no evil in Him. God does not demand a *good try*. He demands *perfection*.

1. *None of us are "good enough."*

We have all sinned and our sins separate us from God. [12] When we try to resolve the problem of our sin in our own strength, we are just like Adam and Eve making clothing from leaves in the Garden. Our attempts to remedy our situation are inadequate.

Our efforts for dealing with the sin in our life (trying to balance out the bad things we do with good things) are not enough. Our "good works" we offer God are like filthy rags in comparison to God's holiness! (**Isaiah 64:6**)

2. *If we got what we "deserved," we would get eternal death.*

God's Word is very clear on the payment for sin. We are sinners and we deserve death![13]

When we begin to understand 1) God's holiness 2) Our sinfulness 3) The seriousness of sin and 4) The payment God requires, then we realize *We do not want what we deserve!*

3. *Salvation is not through "good works"*

When Jesus was asked what the works were that God required, He didn't give them a list of things to do. Jesus didn't say: fasts, pilgrimages, prayers, church attendance, baptism, don't smoke, don't drink, etc. Instead, Jesus told them God required only one thing: *to believe in Him.* (**John 6:28,29**)

Read: Ephesians 2:8,9 - Grace means favor we do not deserve. We cannot earn our salvation by our own good works. All we can do is believe what God has said and accept the life He offers.

See also: **Galatians 2:16** and **Romans 11:6**

---

[12] See number 1 for more on sin.

[13] See number 2.

> ### 5. Do you think you're going to Heaven? (cont.)
> ❏ No, I've sinned too many times.

Read: John 3:14-17 - God did not come to condemn you but to save you!

God reaffirms that He sent Jesus in order to save a sinful world, not condemn it. On the cross, Jesus took all of our condemnation.

All God asks us to do is believe in Jesus and He will give us eternal life, just as God offered life to all of the Israelites in the desert. When the Israelites were bitten by venomous snakes in the wilderness, God offered complete healing to all people, if they would only believe what He said. God did not say, "Those of you who are good may be healed; those of you who have been very bad are going to die from the snakebite!" In the same way, Jesus Christ came to save you.[14]

1. Jesus' Blood was enough for you!

This thief on the cross was mostly likely a murderer who had committed heinous crimes to be given the sentence of crucifixion, yet when He believed in Jesus, Jesus said to Him, "Today you will be with me in paradise." There is no sin that is too great to be forgiven by the blood of Jesus! (Luke 23:42-43)

2. God will not hold your sins against you!

On the cross Jesus shouted, "It is finished[15]!" Jesus had completely accomplished all that was necessary for our salvation. He completely paid for our sins and fulfilled all the requirements of God. Your sins cannot condemn you any longer! (**John 19:30**) The Bible says when God forgives your sins, He removes them as far as the east is from the west. (**Psalm 103:11,12**)

3. Humility or arrogance?

Sometimes we think we are being humble by saying, "I don't think He can save me." In reality however, it is arrogance to look at the Lamb of God and say, "I don't think Your death was sufficient."

---

[14] Just as there was only one way to be healed in the desert, the same is true with the eternal life God offers through Jesus. Rejection of Jesus, is a rejections of the only way to be saved.

[15] Tetelestai in the Greek.

> **5. Do you think you're going to Heaven? (cont.)**
> ❏ I think so, but many times I'm afraid I'm not going to Heaven.

1. **Is your name in the Book of Life?** Read **Revelation 20:12,15** for what God says about this.

   If you <u>believe</u> in Christ:

   If you believe in Jesus Christ then your sins are paid for by Jesus. Because He took your punishment, you are forgiven.[16] Because Jesus has already been judged and condemned in your place, there is no longer any judgment against you! God has given you life! (**Romans 8:1**) When you die, you will be welcomed into God's presence, because your name has been recorded in the Book of Life.

   If you <u>reject</u> Christ:

   If you do *not* believe in Jesus Christ and *do not* accept His death in your place, then your name will *not* be written in the Book of Life. You will still be under the condemnation of your sins because you did not accept that Christ be judged in your place. (**John 3:36**)

   Books will be opened and you will be judged according to what is recorded in the books about your life.[17] If your life is examined by a Holy God, He will give you a just and holy sentence - only what you deserve. The problem is, what you will *deserve* is death.[18]

2. **If you believe in Christ, nothing can separate you from God's love!**
   Read: Romans 8:1; 31-39

   You are completely forgiven. No condemnation can be against you. Nothing can separate you from the love of God that is poured out to you because of Jesus!

---

[16] See number 4, "Jesus died as our Substitute" and "Jesus died to be the final sacrifice for our atonement.""

[17] See number 2, "After death we will give account to God."

[18] See number 5 "What we deserve is death."

> **5. Do you think you're going to Heaven? (cont.)**
> ❑ Absolutely yes! I have no doubts!

God wants you to have certainty! Read: **John 5:24** and **I John 5:13**:

God promises in His Word that you can have the assurance of going to Heaven. If you believe in Jesus then you have crossed over from death to life! You can know for a fact that you have eternal life!

> **6. If you were to die today and stand before God and He were to ask you, "Why should I let you into Heaven?" What would you say?**

A question each person must answer:

The Bible says, "*death is the destiny of everyone; the living should take this to heart.*" (**Ecclesiastes 7:2**) It was intrinsically important for you to answer this question in your own words because each one of us will have to stand before God someday.

In the busyness of life and the pressures of our day to day schedule, many times we don't take time out to consider the most important question of all: What will happen after I die? Where will I go? Am I prepared?

> **7. After finishing this Bible Study:**
> ❑ I'm not sure what to believe. I would like to know more. I have a lot of questions.

If you are still searching and still have unanswered questions, I urge you to continue pursuing the Truth. Continue examining the claims of Jesus Christ.

Talk to your Bible Study leader, get in contact with Light in Action or one of the other ministries that would love to assist you on this journey. Ask God to reveal Himself to you. Don't stop your investigation before coming to a conclusion!

> **7. After finishing this Bible Study: (cont.)**
>
> I believe that Jesus Christ is the Messiah who died for my sins in my place and rose again.
>
> ❏ I was already a believer:

We pray that you have fallen more deeply in love with the One who gave His life for you and that your faith has been strengthened!

Pray that God will give you a renewed boldness for sharing the message of God's love with others! We challenge you to next lead a Bible Study yourself! It doesn't matter whether you start a big group or invite just your neighbor next door, the fact is God has given us the most important message and told us to share the message of eternal life with those who have never heard!

> **7. After finishing this Bible Study: (cont.)**
>
> I believe that Jesus Christ is the Messiah who died for my sins in my place and rose again.
>
> ❏ I believe now.

Maybe as you studied through *Tetelestai* you understood for the first time the message of the Bible and why God sent His Son, Jesus, into the world to die for our sins! You have just made the decision that impacts your eternal destiny, you have chosen LIFE, the life that God offers you through His Son, Jesus. Life that will never end! Welcome to His Family!

CHAPTER 12: WHAT DO YOU BELIEVE?

WE'D LOVE TO HEAR FROM YOU!

If you were strengthened in your faith or became a believer in Jesus Christ after studying *Tetelestai*, the Light in Action team would love to hear from you! You can write to us at the following addresses:

Light in Action Team:

E-mail	Tetelestai@lightinaction.org
Address	Light in Action 1104 El Sonoro Dr. Sierra Vista, AZ, 85635

You can also connect with any of the following ministries below. Let them know you watched *Tetelestai*. They would love to answer your questions and assist you in your journey with God.

Chat with Someone or Ask Questions:

Talk to Someone Live	**Call:** 888-NeedHim (888-633-3446) **Chat Online:** www.chataboutJesus.com
Ask a Question	www.gotquestions.org
Ask a Question	www.everystudent.com
Free Bible Study to help you grow in your relationship with God.	https://www.everystudent.com/features/followup.html

Study Guide Appendix

Why You Can Believe the Bible..117

What are some exciting discoveries in Archaeology?.................129

Who is the Devil?...132

Can the flood mentioned in Genesis be proven?......................136

Is there activity of demonic spirits in the world today?...........138

What is the Christian view of psychics / fortune tellers?.........141

Messianic Prophecies & Fulfillment..143

Is Jesus a Myth? Is Jesus just a copy of the pagan gods of ancient religions?...146

How do we know Jesus ever really lived?...............................151

Did Jesus Really exist? Is there any historical evidence of Jesus Christ?..153

How can a loving God send people to hell?............................156

What Happens Then? Life now. Life then. Life after death?....158

Why Did Jesus Die?...162

Why Should I believe in Christ's resurrection?........................166

Beyond Blind Faith..171

WHY YOU CAN BELIEVE THE BIBLE

It is the history of the Bible that makes it unique among 'sacred texts.' See who wrote the Bible, how its reportive style is backed by archaeology and historians...

History of the Bible - Who wrote the Bible?

The Bible was written over a span of 1500 years, by 40 writers. Unlike other religious writings, the Bible reads as a factual news account of real events, places, people, and dialogue. Historians and archaeologists have repeatedly confirmed its authenticity.

Using the writers' own writing styles and personalities, God shows us who He is and what it's like to know Him. There is one central message consistently carried by all 40 writers of the Bible: God, who created us all, desires a relationship with us. He calls us to know Him and trust Him.

The Bible not only inspires us, it explains life and God to us. It does not answer *all* the questions we might have, but enough of them. It shows us how to live with purpose and compassion. How to relate to others. It encourages us to rely on God for strength, direction, and enjoy His love for us. The Bible also tells us how we can have eternal life.

Multiple categories of evidence support the historical accuracy of the Bible as well as its claim to divine authorship. Here are a few reasons you can trust the Bible.

Archaeology confirms the Bible's historical accuracy.

Archaeologists have consistently discovered the names of government officials, kings, cities, and festivals mentioned in the Bible -- sometimes when historians didn't think such people or places existed. For example, the Gospel of John tells of Jesus healing a cripple next to the Pool of Bethesda. The text even describes the five porticoes (walkways) leading to the pool. Scholars didn't think the pool existed, until archaeologists found it forty feet below ground, complete with the five porticoes.[1]

The Bible has a tremendous amount of historical detail, so not everything mentioned in it has yet been found through archaeology. However, not one archaeological find has conflicted with what the Bible records.[2]
In contrast, news reporter Lee Strobel comments about the *Book of Mormon*: "Archaeology has repeatedly failed to substantiate its claims about events that supposedly occurred long ago in the Americas. I remember writing to the Smithsonian Institute to inquire about whether there was any evidence supporting the claims of

Mormonism, only to be told in unequivocal terms that its archaeologists see 'no direct connection between the archaeology of the New World and the subject matter of the book.'" Archaeologists have never located cities, persons, names, or places mentioned in the *Book of Mormon*.[3]

Many of the ancient locations mentioned by Luke in the Book of Acts in the New Testament, have been identified through archaeology. "In all, Luke names thirty-two countries, fifty-four cities and nine islands without an error."[4]

Archaeology has also refuted many ill-founded theories about the Bible. For example, a theory still taught in some colleges today asserts that Moses could not have written the Pentateuch (the first five books of the Bible), because writing had not been invented in his day. Then archaeologists discovered the Black Stele. "It had wedge-shaped characters on it and contained the detailed laws of Hammurabi. Was it post-Moses? No! It was pre-Mosaic; not only that, but it was pre-Abraham (2,000 B.C.). It preceded Moses' writings by at least three centuries."[5]

Archaeology consistently confirms the historical accuracy of the Bible.

Chart listing some of the major archaeological finds:

ARCHAEOLOGICAL FIND	SIGNIFICANCE
Mari Tablets	Over 20,000 cuneiform tablets, which date back to Abraham's time period, explain many of the patriarchal traditions of Genesis.
Ebla Tablets	Over 20,000 tablets, many containing law similar to the Deuteronomy law code. The previously thought fictitious five cities of the plain in Genesis 14 (Sodom, Gomorrah, Admah, Zeboiim, and Zoar) are identified.
Nuzi Tablets	They detail customs of the 14th and 15th century parallel to the patriarchal accounts such as maids producing children for barren wives.

ARCHAEOLOGICAL FIND	SIGNIFICANCE
Black Stele	Proved that writing and written laws existed three centuries before the Mosaic laws.
Temple Walls of Karnak, Egypt	Signifies a 10th century B.C. reference to Abraham.
Laws of Eshnunna (ca. 1950 B.C.); Lipit-Ishtar Code (ca. 1860 B.C.); Laws of Hammurabi (ca. 1700 B.C.)	Show that the law codes of the Pentateuch were not too sophisticated for that period.
Ras Shamra Tablets	Provide information on Hebrew poetry.
Lachish Letters	Describe Nebuchadnezzar's invasion of Judah and give insight into the time of Jeremiah.
Gedaliah Seal	References Gedaliah is spoken of in 2 Kings 25:22.
Cyrus Cylinder	Authenticates the Biblical description of Cyrus' decree to allow the Jews to rebuild the temple in Jerusalem (see 2 Chronicles 36:23; Ezra 1:2-4).
Moabite Stone	Gives information about Omri, the sixth king of Israel.
Black Obelisk of Shalmaneser III	Illustrates how Jehu, king of Israel, had to submit to the Assyrian king.
Taylor Prism	Contains an Assyrian text which details Sennacherib's attack on Jerusalem during the time of Hezekiah, king of Israel.

PAST CHARGES BY CRITICS	ANSWERED BY ARCHAEOLOGY
Moses could not have written the Pentateuch because he lived before the invention of writing.	Writing existed many centuries before Moses.
Abraham's home city of Ur does not exist.	Ur was discovered. One of the columns had the inscription "Abram."
The city built of solid rock called "Petra" does not exist.	Petra was discovered.
The story of the fall of Jericho is a myth. The city never existed.	The city was found and excavated. It was found that the walls tumbled in the exact manner described by the biblical narrative.
The "Hittites" did not exist.	Hundreds of references to the amazing Hittite civilization have been found. One can even get a doctorate in Hittite studies at the University of Chicago.
Belshazzar was not a real king of Babylon; he is not found in the records.	Tablets of Babylonia describe the reign of this coregent and son of Nabonidus.

The Bible today is the same as what was originally written.

Some people have the idea that the Bible has been translated "so many times" that it has become corrupted through stages of translating. That would probably be true if the translations were being made from other translations. But translations are actually made directly from original Greek, Hebrew and Aramaic source texts based on thousands of ancient manuscripts.

The accuracy of today's Old Testament was confirmed in 1947 when archaeologists found "The Dead Sea Scrolls" along today's West Bank in Israel. "The Dead Sea Scrolls" contained Old Testament scripture dating

1,000 years older than any manuscripts we had. When comparing the manuscripts at hand with these, from 1,000 years earlier, we find agreement 99.5% of the time. And the .5% differences are minor spelling variances and sentence structure that don't change the meaning of the sentence.

Regarding the New Testament, it is humanity's most reliable ancient document. All ancient manuscripts were written on papyrus, which didn't have much of a shelf life. So people hand copied originals, to maintain the message and circulate it to others.

Few people doubt Plato's writing of "The Republic." It's a classic, written by Plato around 380 B.C. The earliest copies we have of it are dated 900 A.D., which is a 1,300 year time lag from when he wrote it. There are only seven copies in existence. Caesar's "Gallic Wars" were written around 100-44 B.C. The copies we have today are dated 1,000 years after he wrote it. We have ten copies.

When it comes to the New Testament, written between 50-100 A.D, there are more than 5,000 copies. All are within 50-225 years of their original writing. Further, when it came to Scripture, scribes (monks) were meticulous in their copying of original manuscripts. They checked and rechecked their work, to make sure it perfectly matched. What the New Testament writers originally wrote is preserved better than any other ancient manuscript.

We can be more certain of what we read about Jesus' life and words, than we are certain of the writings of Caesar, Plato, Aristotle and Homer.

A comparison of the New Testament to other ancient writings:

Author	Book	Date Written	Earliest Copies	Time Gap	# of Copies
Homer	*Iliad*	800 B.C.	c. 400 B.C.	c. 400 yrs.	643
Herodotus	*History*	480-425 B.C.	c. A.D. 900	c. 1,350 yrs.	8

Author	Book	Date Written	Earliest Copies	Time Gap	# of Copies
Thucydides	*History*	460-400 B.C.	c. A.D. 900	c. 1,300 yrs.	8
Plato		400 B.C.	c. A.D. 900	c. 1,300 yrs.	7
Demosthenes		300 B.C.	c. A.D. 1100	c. 1,400 yrs.	200
Caesar	*Gallic Wars*	100-44 B.C.	c. A.D. 900	c. 1,000 yrs.	10
Tacitus	*Annals*	A.D. 100	c. A.D. 1100	c. 1,000 yrs.	20
Pliny Secundus	*Natural History*	A.D. 61-113	c. A.D. 850	c. 750 yrs.	7
New Testament		A.D. 50-100	c. A.D. 114 (portions) c. A.D. 200 (books) c. A.D. 325 (complete N.T.)	c. +50 yrs. c. 100 yrs. c. 225 yrs.	5366

More reasons to trust the gospel accounts of Jesus.

Four of the writers of the New Testament each wrote their own biography on the life of Jesus. These are called the four gospels, the first four books of the New Testament. When historians try to determine if a biography is reliable, they ask, "How many other sources report the same details about this person?"

Here's how this works. Imagine you are collecting biographies of President John F. Kennedy. You find many biographies describing his family, his presidency, his goal of putting a man on the moon, and his handling of the Cuban Missile Crisis. Regarding Jesus, do we find multiple biographies reporting similar facts about his life? Yes.

Here is a sampling of facts about Jesus, and where you would find that fact reported in each of their biographies.

	Matthew	Mark	Luke	John
Jesus was born of a virgin	1:18-25	-	1:27, 34	-
He was born in Bethlehem	2:1	-	2:4	-
He lived in Nazareth	2:23	1:9, 24	2:51, 4:16	1:45, 46
Jesus was baptized by John the Baptist	3:1-15	1:4-9	3:1-22	-
He performed miracles of healing	4:24, etc.	1:34, etc.	4:40, etc.	9:7
He walked on water	14:25	6:48	-	6:19
He fed five thousand people with five loaves and two fish	14:7	6:38	9:13	6:9
Jesus taught the common people	5:1	4:25, 7:28	9:11	18:20
He spent time with social outcasts	9:10, 21:31	2:15, 16	5:29, 7:29	8:3
He argued with the religious elite	15:7	7:6	12:56	8:1-58
The religious elite plotted to kill him	12:14	3:6	19:47	11:45-57
They handed Jesus over to the Romans	27:1, 2	15:1	23:1	18:28
Jesus was flogged	27:26	15:15	-	19:1

He was crucified	27:26-50	15:22-37	23:33-46	19:16-30
He was buried in a tomb	27:57-61	15:43-47	23:50-55	19:38-42
Jesus rose from the dead and appeared to his followers	28:1-20	16:1-20	24:1-53	20:1-31

Two of the gospel biographies were written by the apostles Matthew and John, men who knew Jesus personally and traveled with him for over three years. The other two books were written by Mark and Luke, close associates of the apostles. These writers had direct access to the facts they were recording. At the time of their writing, there were still people alive who had heard Jesus speak, watched him heal people and perform miracles.

So the early church readily accepted the four gospels because they agreed with what was already common knowledge about Jesus' life.

Each of the gospels of Matthew, Mark, Luke and John, read like news reports, factual accountings of the days' events, each from their own perspective. The descriptions are unique to each writer, but the facts are in agreement.

Sample of what is presented in one of the Gospels...

The Gospels are presented as matter-of-fact, "this is how it was." Even reports of Jesus doing the miraculous are written without sensationalism or mysticism. One typical example is the account in Luke, chapter 8, where Jesus brings a little girl back to life.

Notice the details and clarity in its reporting:

Then a man named Jairus, a ruler of the synagogue, came and fell at Jesus' feet, pleading with Him to come to his house because his only daughter, a girl of about twelve, was dying.

As Jesus was on his way, the crowds almost crushed Him. And a woman was there who had been subject to bleeding for twelve years, but no one could heal her.

She came up behind Him and touched the edge of his cloak, and immediately her bleeding stopped.

"Who touched me?" Jesus asked. When they all denied it, Peter said, "Master, the people are crowding and pressing against you." But Jesus said, "Someone touched me; I know that power has gone out from me."

Then the woman, seeing that she could not go unnoticed, came trembling and fell at his feet. In the presence of all the people, she told why she had touched Him and how she had been instantly healed. Then He said to her, "Daughter, your faith has healed you. Go in peace."

While Jesus was still speaking, someone came from the house of Jairus, the synagogue ruler. "Your daughter is dead," he said. "Don't bother the teacher any more." Hearing this, Jesus said to Jairus, "Don't be afraid; just believe, and she will be healed."

When He arrived at the house of Jairus, He did not let anyone go in with Him except Peter, John and James, and the child's father and mother. Meanwhile, all the people were wailing and mourning for her. "Stop wailing," Jesus said. "She is not dead but asleep." They laughed at Him, knowing that she was dead.
But He took her by the hand and said, "My child, get up!" Her spirit returned, and at once she stood up. Then Jesus told them to give her something to eat. Her parents were astonished, but He ordered them not to tell anyone what had happened.

Like other accounts of Jesus healing people, this has a ring of authenticity. If it were fiction, there are portions of it that would have been written differently. For example, in a fictional account there wouldn't be an interruption with something else happening. If it were fiction, the people in mourning would not have laughed at Jesus' statement; get angry maybe, be hurt by it, but not laugh. And in writing fiction, would Jesus have ordered the parents to be quiet about it? You would expect the healing to make a grand point. But real life isn't always smooth. There are interruptions. People do react oddly. And Jesus had his own reasons for not wanting the parents to broadcast this.

The best test of the Gospels' authenticity is to read it for yourself. Does it read like a report of real events, or like fiction? If it is real, then God has revealed Himself to us. Jesus came, lived, taught, inspired, and brought life to millions who read His words and life today. What Jesus stated in the gospels, many have found reliably true: "I have come that they might have life, and have it more abundantly." (John 10:10)

Here's why the gospels were written.

In the early years after Jesus' death and resurrection there was no apparent need for written biographies about Jesus. Those living in the Jerusalem region were witnesses of Jesus and well aware of his ministry.[6]
However, when news of Jesus spread beyond Jerusalem, and the eyewitnesses were no longer readily accessible, there was a need for written accounts to educate others about Jesus' life and ministry.

If you would like to know more about Jesus, this article will give you a good summary of his life: Beyond Blind Faith. Pg. 171

How the books of the New Testament were determined.

The early church accepted the New Testament books almost as soon as they were written. It's already been mentioned that the writers were friends of Jesus or His immediate followers, men to whom Jesus had entrusted the leadership of the early church. The Gospel writers Matthew and John were some of Jesus' closest followers.

Mark and Luke were companions of the apostles, having access to the apostles' account of Jesus' life. The other New Testament writers had immediate access to Jesus as well: James and Jude were half-brothers of Jesus who initially did not believe in Him. Peter was one of the 12 apostles. Paul started out as a violent opponent of Christianity and a member of the religious ruling class, but he became an ardent follower of Jesus, convinced that Jesus rose from the dead.

The reports in the New Testament books lined up with what thousands of eyewitnesses had seen for themselves. When other books were written hundreds of years later, it wasn't difficult for the church to spot them as forgeries. For example, the Gospel of Judas was written by the Gnostic sect, around 130-170 A.D., long after Judas' death. The Gospel of Thomas, written around 140 A.D., is another example of a counterfeit writing erroneously bearing an apostle's name.

These and other Gnostic gospels conflicted with the known teachings of Jesus and the Old Testament, and often contained numerous historical and geographical errors.[7] In A.D. 367, Athanasius formally listed the 27 New Testament books (the same list that we have today). Soon after, Jerome and Augustine circulated this same list. These lists, however, were not necessary for the majority of Christians. By and large, the whole church had recognized and used the same list of books since the first century after Christ.

As the church grew beyond the Greek-speaking lands and needed to translate the Scriptures, and as splinter sects continued to pop up with their own competing holy books, it became more important to have a definitive list.

Historians confirm what the Bible says about Jesus.

Not only do we have well-preserved copies of the original manuscripts, we also have testimony from both Jewish and Roman historians.

The gospels report that Jesus of Nazareth performed many miracles, was executed by the Romans, and rose from the dead. Numerous ancient historians back the Bible's account of the life of Jesus and his followers: Cornelius Tacitus (A.D. 55-120), an historian of first-century Rome, is considered one of the most accurate historians of the ancient world.[8] An excerpt from Tacitus tells us that the Roman emperor Nero "inflicted the most exquisite tortures on a class...called Christians. ...Christus [Christ], from whom the name had its origin, suffered the extreme penalty during the reign of Tiberius at the hands of one of our procurators, Pontius Pilatus...."[9]

Flavius Josephus, a Jewish historian (A.D. 38-100), wrote about Jesus in his *Jewish Antiquities*. From Josephus, "we learn that Jesus was a wise man who did surprising feats, taught many, won over followers from among Jews and Greeks, was believed to be the Messiah, was accused by the Jewish leaders, was condemned to be crucified by Pilate, and was considered to be resurrected."[10]

Suetonius, Pliny the Younger, and Thallus also wrote about Christian worship and persecution that is consistent with New Testament accounts.

Even the Jewish *Talmud,* certainly not biased toward Jesus, concurs about the major events of his life. From the *Talmud,* "we learn that Jesus was conceived out of wedlock, gathered disciples, made blasphemous claims about himself, and worked miracles, but these miracles are attributed to sorcery and not to God."[11]

This is remarkable information considering that most ancient historians focused on political and military leaders, not on obscure rabbis from distant provinces of the Roman Empire. Yet ancient historians (Jews, Greeks and Romans) confirm the major events that are presented in the New Testament, even though they were not believers themselves.

Does it matter if Jesus really did and said what is in the Gospels?

Yes. For faith to really be of any value, it must be based on facts, on reality. Here is why. If you were taking a flight to London, you would probably have faith that the jet is fueled and mechanically reliable, the pilot trained, and no terrorists are on board. Your faith, however, is not what gets you to London. Your faith is useful in that it got you on the plane. But what actually gets you to London is the integrity of the plane, pilot, etc. You could rely on your positive experience of past flights. But your positive experience would not be enough to get that plane to London. What matters is the object of your faith -- is it reliable?

Is the New Testament an accurate, reliable presentation of Jesus? Yes. We can trust the New Testament because there is enormous factual support for it. This article touched on the following points: historians concur, archaeology concurs, the four Gospel biographies are in agreement, the preservation of document copies is remarkable, there is superior accuracy in the translations. All of this gives a solid foundation for believing that what we read today is what the original writers wrote and experienced in real life, in real places.
John, one of the writers, sums it up well, "Now Jesus did many other signs in the presence of the disciples, which are not written in this book; but these are written so that you may believe that Jesus is the Christ, the Son of God, and that by believing you may have life in His name."[12]

Footnotes: (1) Strobel, Lee. *The Case for Christ* (Zondervan Publishing House, 1998), p. 132. (2) The renowned Jewish archaeologist, Nelson Glueck, wrote: "It may be stated categorically that no archaeological discovery has ever controverted a biblical reference." cited by McDowell, Josh. (3) Strobel, p. 143-144. (4) Geisler, Norman L. *Baker Encyclopedia of Christian Apologetics* (Grand Rapids: Baker, 1998). (5) McDowell, Josh. *Evidence That Demands a Verdict* (1972), p. 19. (6) See Acts 2:22, 3:13, 4:13, 5:30, 5:42, 6:14, etc. (7) Bruce, F.F. *The Books and the Parchments: How We Got Our English Bible* (Fleming H. Revell Co., 1950), p. 113. (8) McDowell, Josh. *The New Evidence that Demands a Verdict* (Thomas Nelson Publishers, 1999), p. 55. (9) Tacitus, A. 15.44. (10) Wilkins, Michael J. & Moreland, J.P. *Jesus Under Fire* (Zondervan Publishing House, 1995), p. 40. (11) Ibid. (12) John 20:30,31

Used with Permission from EveryStudent

https://www.everystudent.com/features/bible.html

WHAT ARE SOME EXCITING DISCOVERIES IN BIBLICAL ARCHAEOLOGY?

Answer: Biblical archaeology is the science of investigating and recovering remains of past cultures that can validate, or at least shed new light on, the biblical narrative. Biblical archaeology involves the study of architecture, language, literature, art, tools, pottery and many other items that have survived the ravages of time. For almost two hundred years, those who study biblical archaeology have been working in the Middle East in their quest to recover the past. There have been thousands of archaeological finds that have advanced the study greatly, but some are more significant than others. Some of these finds have been the Dead Sea Scrolls, the Tel Dan Inscription, the Caiaphas Ossuary, the Crucified Man, the Ketef Hinnom Amulets, the House of God Ostracon, and the Pilate Inscription. Let's briefly look at each one of these to see why they are significant.

Dead Sea Scrolls: One of the most important finds in the field of biblical archaeology is the discovery of the Dead Sea Scrolls in 1947 in the Qumran area on the northwest shore of the Dead Sea. There are approximately 900 documents and fragments that comprise the find. The scrolls predate A.D. 100 and include a complete copy of the book of Isaiah. The significance of the find is the age of the documents and the astonishing lack of variants to documents that have been most trustworthy such as the Masoretic Text, Codex Vaticanus and the Codex Sinaiticus. The vast majority of the variants (about 99 percent) are punctuation or spelling errors. Incredibly, none of the variants changed the meaning of the text, nor did they contain any significant theological differences. This gives us the assurance that the text we have today in our Bible is the same as the early church had two thousand years ago. No other secular manuscripts can make the same claim.

Tel Dan Inscription: This stone tablet contains an inscription that is the first reference to the Davidic dynasty outside of the Bible. It was erected by Hazael, king of Aram, which is present-day Syria. The inscription makes reference to a military victory and corresponds to the biblical account in 2 Chronicles 22. This inscription dates to the 9th century B.C., thus giving us accurate dating to the Davidic dynasty as well verifying its existence. This is the only extra-biblical reference to the House of David that has been discovered to date.

Caiaphas Ossuary: An ossuary is a stone or pottery box in which the remains of a deceased person are buried (an ancient casket). The Caiaphas Ossuary bears the inscription "*Yeosef bar Qafa*" and is dated to the second temple period. Yeosef (Joseph) was the son of Caiaphas. This verifies that there was a high priest at the time of Jesus and his name was Caiaphas. Caiaphas was the priest that presided over the false trial of Jesus (Matthew 26:57-67).

Crucified Man: This is the remains of a full skeleton of a man crucified in the first century. The foot bone contains a bent crucifixion nail. There have been those that argued that the crucifixion of Christ was a hoax because that was not a form of capital punishment in Christ's time. These remains verify that crucifixion was being done and that the crucifixion of Jesus was done exactly as outlined in the biblical narrative.

Ketef Hinnom Amulets: In 1979, two silver scrolls that were worn as amulets were found in a tomb at Ketef Hinnom, overlooking the Hinnom Valley, where they had been placed around the 7th century B.C. The delicate process of unrolling the scrolls while developing a method that would prevent them from disintegrating took three years. Brief as they are, the amulets rank as the oldest surviving texts from the Hebrew Bible. Upon unrolling the amulets, biblical archaeologists found two inscriptions of significance. One is a temple priest blessing from the book of Numbers: "The Lord bless you and protect you. The Lord make his face to shine upon you and be gracious to you. The Lord lift up his countenance to you and give you peace" (Numbers 6:24-26). The other is the tetragrammaton *YHWH*, the name of the Lord, from which we get the English *Jehovah*. The amulets predate the Dead Sea Scrolls by 500 years and are the oldest known example of the Lord's name in writing.

House of God Ostracon: Ostraca—writings on pottery—are common finds in archaeological digs. The House of God Ostracon was found in Arad, a Canaanite city in the Negev. Over 100 pieces of ostraca were found and have been dated to the early part of the 6th Century BC. Of significance are the references to the temple in Jerusalem and to names of people that are recorded in Scripture. This not only helps to date the temple, but it verifies the existence of people listed in the biblical text.

Pilate Inscription: This stone tablet was found in Caesarea on the Mediterranean coast. The tablet was found in the theater of Caesarea and bears an inscription mentioning the name of Pontius Pilate the procurator of Judea, and the Tiberium, which was an edifice built in honor of the Emperor Tiberius by Pilate. There has been much written to discredit the biblical narrative in regard to the existence of Pilate; this tablet clearly says that it was from "Pontius Pilate, Prefect of Judea" and verifies that he was a person that lived during the time of Jesus, exactly as written in the biblical narrative.

These finds are interesting from an educational point of view and do validate the historical accuracy of the Bible. But for the believer, finds like these should add nothing to our understanding of the importance or credibility of the Bible. The Bible is the written Word of God, inerrant and infallible and was God-breathed to human writers and is useful for edifying and teaching believers in the ways of God: "All Scripture is God-breathed and is useful for teaching, rebuking, correcting and training in righteousness, so that the man of God may be thoroughly equipped for every good work" (2 Timothy 3:16-17). The Bible needs no corroborative evidence to verify its truth, but it is interesting to note that no scientific or archaeological find has ever disproven a single word of Scripture, and many, many findings have attested to its historical and scientific accuracy.

Recommended Resource: The Popular Handbook of Archaeology and the Bible by Geisler & Holden

---

Used with Permission from GotQuestions

https://www.gotquestions.org/biblical-archaeology.html

STUDY GUIDE APPENDIX

WHO IS THE DEVIL?

A brief description of the devil. Who is he? And is he a threat to you?

In cartoons and comics, the devil appears as a cute, benign tempter, pushing you to do something that's fun or a little bit wrong. In reality however, Satan is anything but cute.

Who is the devil? He is not God's counterpart, because God has no equal, no opposite. God has always existed, and everything else that exists now, including angels, were created by God.

The devil (sometimes referred to as Satan or Lucifer) is an angel who rebelled against God. He is the enemy not only of God, but also of humankind, relentless in his mission: to kill, destroy, or enslave us. We're warned, "...be watchful. Your adversary the devil prowls around like a roaring lion, seeking someone to devour."[1]

The devil's power is laughable compared to the power of God. Yet, he is a real threat to humans, and has the capacity to ruin a person's life.

Satan has one primary tactic: to deceive us. He seeks to deceive entire nations, the world, and individuals. He twists and distorts what is true, and there is power in his lies.

Dr. Neil Anderson made an astute observation. He said the Bible describes Satan in three ways:
- The tempter
- The accuser
- The father of lies

Dr. Anderson noted, "If I were to tempt you, you would know it. If I were to accuse you, you would know it. But if I were to deceive you, you wouldn't know it. The power of Satan is in the lie. If you remove the lie you remove the power."

In what ways does the devil lie?

Here are just a few examples.
God created Adam and Eve with free will to choose and make decisions, just like humans can today. The Garden of Eden contained perhaps hundreds of fruit-bearing trees. The only instruction God gave to Adam and Eve was to not eat from one particular tree. It was a straightforward instruction to follow. Just don't eat from that one tree or you will die. Simple enough.

Yet Satan persuaded Eve, "You will not surely die." That's the initial lie. Now he lies further, "You will not surely die. For God knows that when you eat of it your eyes will be opened, and you will be like God, knowing good and evil."[2]

Satan deceived Eve, convincing her that God was withholding something wonderful from them, that this fruit would make them like God. And wouldn't that be a good thing? The problem was, it wasn't true. Adam and Eve believed Satan's lie, rather than what God told them, leading to horrible consequences. That's exactly how the devil operates. He distorts the truth in order to harm the person.

How the Devil Accuses God

Satan's greatest desire is to keep people far away from God. He will seek to either cause you to deny God's existence or to slander, lie about God's character. Here's an example.

God repeatedly affirms his love for us. "I have loved you with an everlasting love, therefore I have continued my faithfulness to you."[3] "...not that we loved God, but that he loved us..."[4] "See what kind of love the Father has given to us..."[5] "For God so loved the world that He gave His only Son, that whoever believes in Him should not perish, but have eternal life."[6]

But what does Satan say? "God doesn't love you. Look at all the problems you have. If God loved you, you wouldn't have these problems." Sounds convincing.

Yet all people face problems. It's part of life. What Satan neglects to tell you is that if you have a relationship with God and depend on Him, God can lead you through those problems. You do not need to shoulder or solve them on your own. God can give you wisdom and real strength in the midst of those problems. Not only that, but He says while we face difficulties, "...my peace I give to you..."[7] Why? Because the person knows that God can be trusted.

Without God, a person is described as "without hope in this world." That is not God's desire for anyone.

How the Devil Accuses You

Not only does Satan try to deceive you about God's goodness, but Satan also slanders you to God. Satan did this with a man named Job. Satan said if Job suffered, then Job would curse God to His face, which Job never did. Satan seeks to undermine you and condemn you before God.

But not only that. Satan turns his slander and condemnation toward you.

He convinces you, "God wouldn't want you. You could never be holy enough. Look at all the junk in your life, all the ways you've failed, the things you do, the addictions you have. God would never accept you or want you. You'd never make it."

Again, all lies. God is very clear that none of us need to become "good" in order to be accepted by God, nor to become sinless in order to maintain that relationship with God.

Jesus said of Satan, "He was a murderer from the beginning...there is no truth in him. When he lies, he speaks out of his own character, for he is a liar and the father of lies."[8] The contrast between the devil and God is stunning. Jesus said, "The thief comes only to steal and kill and destroy. I came that they may have life and have it abundantly."[9] Jesus says of those who believe in Him, "If you abide in my word...you will know the truth, and the truth will set you free."[10]

Instead of being deceived by Satan, there is an opportunity to know what God says is true about Himself, about your life, about relationships. While Satan would like you to be enslaved by his deception, God wants you to know what's true, to be free and experience real life.

In addition to being a liar and an accuser, Satan, through his lies, tempts people toward slavery and addictions. "Oh go ahead. One more won't hurt you. No one will find out. You're not really hurting anyone. And you'll feel so much better."

How to Deal with Satan

If you decide to begin a relationship with God, you will still be tempted by Satan. You still have free will, making whatever decision you'd like to make. However, in many situations you would also know what's true and be less likely to give in to Satan's lies, less likely to feel helpless, confused or fearful. Further, God offers His help.

We're told, "The temptations in your life are no different from what others experience. And God is faithful. He will not allow the temptation to be more than you can stand. When you are tempted, He will show you a way out so that you can endure."[11]

Who is Satan? A tempter, slanderer, and liar. His intent is to keep people isolated from God, so they will listen only to Satan, joining in his rebellion and experiencing destruction. Nothing he says about God or your life is true.

God desires a relationship with you and for you to experience His love. He created you not to live in darkness and confusion, but to know what's true. Jesus said, "I am the light of the world. Whoever follows Me will not walk in darkness, but will have the light of life."[12]

Footnotes: (1) 1Peter 5:8 (2) Genesis 3:4,5 (3) Jeremiah 31:3 (4) 1John 4:10 (5) 1John 3:1 (6) John 3:16 (7) John 14:27 (8) John 8:44 (9) John 10:10 (10) John 8:31 (11) 1Corinthians 10:13 (12) John 8:12

Used with Permission from EveryStudent

https://www.everystudent.com/wires/devil.html

STUDY GUIDE APPENDIX

CAN THE FLOOD MENTIONED IN GENESIS BE PROVEN?

Is there evidence for the biblical account of a global flood?

Answer: The flood recorded in Genesis 6 cannot be proved with absolute certainty, but there is ample evidence to support the view that a global flood did occur. The Bible presents the flood as part of the early history of the world, yet there are certainly skeptics that will reject the evidence.

One evidence of the flood of Noah's day is the abundance of global flood stories found in a wide variety of cultures. Anthropologists have catalogued hundreds of ancient flood legends from all over the world. The ancient Babylonians, Native Americans, Australian Aboriginals, Aztecs, Romans, Greeks, Chinese, Mayans, Inuits, and many others recorded flood stories. Further, their stories share many similarities to the Genesis account, including an angry god and people who survived the flood in a boat.

A second area of evidence for the flood of Genesis 6 is physical evidence found on the earth's surface. For example, 75 percent of earth's land surface is comprised of sedimentary rock—rock that was washed away, dissolved in fluid, and redeposited elsewhere. Fossils are found in many of these sedimentary layers. It is common to find massive fossil graveyards consisting of jumbled, smashed, and contorted fossil remains that give the appearance of a large number of animals destroyed simultaneously by an incredible force.

A third area of evidence for the flood of Noah's day is the long-distance movement of various types of rock. For example, scientists have noted quartzites discovered more than 300 miles from their source in Oregon, a phenomenon no longer taking place today. The displaced minerals could be the result of what is spoken of in Psalm 104:6–8—the waters standing above the mountains and violently running down into the valleys.

A fourth line of evidence for the global flood is the presence of abundant fossil remains of marine life at the tops of every major mountain range in the world, including the Himalayas. What could have caused this phenomenon? A global flood in which water covered the tallest mountains could explain it. Genesis 7:18–19 notes that "the waters rose and increased greatly on the earth, and the ark floated on the surface of the water. They rose greatly on the earth, and all the high mountains under the entire heavens were covered." Scientists have yet to provide an adequate alternative theory for the abundance of fossilized marine life at high elevations.

The Bible itself serves as an additional line of support. Time and again, the history of the Bible has been validated through a variety of means. If Scripture is accurate in many other areas of history, why would its account of a global flood be disputed? Taken alongside the evidence from the various global flood narratives, abundant fossils, and high-elevation marine fossils, the Bible's account offers a plausible scenario for what took place during the time of Noah.

Recommended Resource: The Genesis Flood: The Biblical Record and Its Scientific Implications, 50th Anniversary Edition by Morris & Whitcomb

---

Used with Permission from GotQuestions

https://www.gotquestions.org/Genesis-flood-proven.html

STUDY GUIDE APPENDIX

IS THERE ACTIVITY OF DEMONIC SPIRITS IN THE WORLD TODAY?

Answer: Ghosts, hauntings, séances, tarot cards, Ouija boards, crystal balls—what do they have in common? They are fascinating to many people because they seem to offer insight into an unknown world that lies beyond the limits of our physical existence. And to many, such things seem innocent and harmless.

Many who approach these subjects from non-biblical perspectives believe that ghosts are the spirits of dead people who, for whatever reason, have not gone on to the "next stage." According to those who believe in ghosts, there are three different kinds of hauntings: (1) residual hauntings (likened to video playbacks with no actual interaction with any spirits). (2) Hauntings by human spirits, whose natures are a combination of good and bad (but not evil). Such spirits may simply want to get a person's attention; others may be pranksters, but, in either case, they do not truly harm people. (3) Interaction with non-human spirits or demons. These entities can masquerade as human spirits, but they are harmful and dangerous.

When reading about ghosts and hauntings from non-biblical sources, remember that, just because an author may refer to the Bible or to Bible characters (such as Michael the archangel), it does not mean he approaches the subject from a biblical perspective. When no authority is given for an author's information, the reader has to ask himself, "How does he/she know this to be so? What is his/her authority?" For example, how does an author know that demons masquerade as human spirits? Ultimately, those who address such subjects from non-biblical sources must base their understanding on their own thoughts, the thoughts of others, and/or the experiences of the past. However, based on their own admission that demons are deceiving and can imitate benevolent human spirits, experiences can be deceiving! If one is to have a right understanding on this subject, he must go to a source that has shown itself to be accurate 100 percent of the time—God's Word, the Bible. Let's take a look at what the Bible has to say about such things.

1. The Bible never speaks of hauntings. Rather, it teaches that when a person dies, the spirit of that person goes to one of two places. If the person is a believer in Jesus Christ, his spirit is ushered into the presence of the Lord in heaven (Philippians 1:21-23; 2 Corinthians 5:8). Later, he will be reunited with his body at the resurrection (1 Thessalonians 4:13-18). If the person is not a believer in Christ, his spirit is put in a place of torment called hell (Luke 16:23-24).

IS THERE ACTIVITY OF DEMONIC SPIRITS IN THE WORLD TODAY?

Whether a person is a believer or an unbeliever, there is no returning to our world to communicate or interact with people, even for the purpose of warning people to flee from the judgment to come (Luke 16:27-31). There are only two recorded incidents in which a dead person interacted with the living. The first is when King Saul of Israel tried contacting the deceased prophet Samuel through a medium. God allowed Samuel to be disturbed long enough to pronounce judgment upon Saul for his repeated disobedience (1 Samuel 28:6-19). The second incident is when Moses and Elijah interacted with Jesus when he was transfigured in Matthew 17:1-8. There was nothing "ghostly" about the appearance of Moses and Elijah, however.

2. Scripture speaks repeatedly of angels moving about unseen (Daniel 10:1-21). Sometimes, these angels have interaction with living people. Evil spirits, or demons, can actually possess people, dwelling within them and controlling them (see Mark 5:1-20, for example). The four Gospels and the Book of Acts record several instances of demon possession and of good angels appearing to and aiding believers. Angels, both good and bad, can cause supernatural phenomena to occur (Job 1–2; Revelation 7:1; 8:5; 15:1;16).

3. Scripture shows that demons know things of which people are unaware (Acts 16:16-18; Luke 4:41). Because these evil angels have been around a long time, they would naturally know things that those living limited life spans would not. Because Satan currently has access to God's presence (Job 1–2), demons might also be allowed to know some specifics about the future, but this is speculation.

4. Scripture says Satan is the father of lies and a deceiver (John 8:44; 2 Thessalonians 2:9) and that he disguises himself as an "angel of light." Those who follow him, human or otherwise, practice the same deceit (2 Corinthians 11:13-15).

5. Satan and demons have great power (compared to humans). Even Michael the archangel trusts only God's power when dealing with Satan (Jude 1:9). But Satan's power is nothing compared to God's (Acts 19:11-12; Mark 5:1-20), and God is able to use Satan's evil intent to bring about His good purposes (1 Corinthians 5:5; 2 Corinthians 12:7).

6. God commands us to have nothing to do with the occult, devil worship, or the unclean spirit world. This would include the use of mediums, séances, Ouija boards, horoscopes, tarot cards, channeling, etc. God considers these practices an abomination (Deuteronomy 18:9-12; Isaiah 8:19-20; Galatians 5:20; Revelation 21:8), and those who involve themselves in such things invite disaster (Acts 19:13-16).

7. The Ephesian believers set an example in dealing with occult items (books, music, jewelry, games, etc.). They confessed their involvement with such as sin and burned the items publicly (Acts 19:17-19).

8. Release from Satan's power is achieved through God's salvation. Salvation comes through believing in the gospel of Jesus Christ (Acts 19:18; 26:16-18). Attempts to disentangle oneself from demonic involvement without salvation are futile. Jesus warned of a heart devoid of the Holy Spirit's presence: such a heart is merely an empty dwelling place ready for even worse demons to inhabit (Luke 11:24-26). But when a person comes to Christ for the forgiveness of sin, the Holy Spirit comes to abide until the day of redemption (Ephesians 4:30).

Some paranormal activity can be attributed to the work of charlatans. It would seem best to understand other reports of ghosts and hauntings as the work of demons. Sometimes these demons may make no attempt to conceal their nature, and at other times they may use deception, appearing as disembodied human spirits. Such deception leads to more lies and confusion.

God states it is foolish to consult the dead on behalf of the living. Rather, He says, "To the law and to the testimony!" (Isaiah 8:19-20). The Word of God is our source of wisdom. Believers in Jesus Christ should not be involved in the occult. The spirit world is real, but Christians do not need to fear it (1 John 4:4).

Recommended Resource: Unseen Realities: Heaven, Hell, Angels, and Demons by R.C. Sproul

Used with Permission from GotQuestions

https://www.gotquestions.org/demonic-activity.html

WHAT IS THE CHRISTIAN VIEW OF PSYCHICS / FORTUNE TELLERS?

Answer: The Bible strongly condemns spiritism, mediums, the occult, and psychics (Leviticus 20:27; Deuteronomy 18:10-13). Horoscopes, tarot cards, astrology, fortune tellers, palm readings, and séances fall into this category as well. These practices are based on the concept that there are gods, spirits, or deceased loved ones that can give advice and guidance. These "gods" or "spirits" are demons (2 Corinthians 11:14-15). The Bible gives us no reason to believe that deceased loved ones can contact us. If they were believers, they are in heaven enjoying the most wonderful place imaginable in fellowship with a loving God. If they were not believers, they are in hell, suffering the un-ending torment for rejecting God's love and rebelling against Him.

So, if our loved ones cannot contact us, how do mediums, spiritists, and psychics get such accurate information? There have been many exposures of psychics as frauds. It has been proven that psychics can gain immense amounts of information on someone through ordinary means. Sometimes by just using a telephone number through caller ID and an internet search, a psychic can get names, addresses, dates of birth, dates of marriage, family members, etc. However, it is undeniable that psychics sometimes know things that should be impossible for them to know. Where do they get this information? The answer is from Satan and his demons. "And no wonder, for Satan himself masquerades as an angel of light. It is not surprising, then, if his servants masquerade as servants of righteousness. Their end will be what their actions deserve" (2 Corinthians 11:14-15). Acts 16:16-18 describes a fortune teller who was able to predict the future until the apostle Paul rebuked a demon out of her.

Satan pretends to be kind and helpful. He tries to appear as something good. Satan and his demons will give a psychic information about a person in order to get that person hooked into spiritism, something that God forbids. It appears innocent at first, but soon people can find themselves addicted to psychics and unwittingly allow Satan to control and destroy their lives.

Peter proclaimed, "Be self-controlled and alert. Your enemy the devil prowls around like a roaring lion looking for someone to devour" (1 Peter 5:8). In some cases, the psychics themselves are deceived, not knowing the true source of the information they receive. Whatever the case and wherever the source of the information, nothing connected to spiritism, witchcraft, or astrology is a godly means of discovering information. How does God want us to discern His will for our life? God's plan is simple, yet powerful and effective: study the Bible (2 Timothy 3:16-17) and pray for wisdom (James 1:5).

Recommended Resource: The Truth Behind Ghosts, Mediums, and Psychic Phenomena by Ron Rhodes

---

Used with Permission from GotQuestions

https://www.gotquestions.org/psychics-Christian.html

MESSIANIC PROPHECIES & FULFILLMENTS:

Messiah Would:	*Prophecy Given:*	*Fulfillment:*
Be born in Bethlehem	Mic. 5:2	Matt. 2:1-6; Lk. 2:1-20
Be born of a virgin	Is. 7:14	Matt. 1:18-25; Lk. 1:26-38
Be a descendant of David	Is. 9:7	Matt. 1:1
Flee to Egypt	Hos. 11:1	Matt. 2:13
Have a forerunner	Is. 40:3	Matt. 1:17; Lk 1:16-17; Jn. 1:19-28
Be a prophet like Moses	Deut. 18:15, 18-19	Jn. 7:40
Enter Jerusalem on a donkey	Zech. 9:9	Matt. 21:1-9; Jn. 12:12-16
Be rejected by His own people	Is. 53:1, 3; Ps. 118:22	Matt. 26:3, 4; Jn. 12:37-43; Acts 4:1-12
Be betrayed by a friend	Ps. 41:9	Matt. 26:14-16, 47-50; Lk. 22:19-23
Be sold for 30 pieces of silver and the silver would be used to buy a field	Zech. 11:12-13	Matt. 26:14-15
Be tried and condemned	Is. 53:8	Lk. 23:1-25; Matt. 27:1,2
Be silent before His accusers	Is. 53:7	Matt. 27:12-14; Mk. 15:3-4; Lk. 23:8-10
Be struck and spat on by His enemies	Is. 50:6	Matt. 26:67; Matt. 27:30; Mk. 14:65

Messiah Would:	Prophecy Given:	Fulfillment:
Be mocked and insulted	Ps. 22:7-8	Matt. 27:39-44; Lk. 23:11, 35
Suffer with criminals	Is. 53:12	Matt. 27:38; Mk. 15:27-28; Lk. 23:32-34
Pray for His enemies	Is. 53:12	Matt. 27:38; Mk. 15:27-28; Lk. 23:32-34
Be given vinegar and gall	Ps. 69:21	Matt. 27:34; Jn. 19:28-30
Have people gamble for His garments	Ps. 22:18	Matt. 27:35; Jn. 19:23-24
Not have any bones broken	Ex. 12:46	Jn. 19:31-36
Die as a sacrifice for sin	Is. 53:5-6, 8, 10-12	Jn. 1:29; 11:49-52; Acts 10:43; 13:38-39
Have His hands and feet pierced	Ps. 22:14, 16-17	Matt. 27:31; Mk. 15:20, 25
Be buried with the rich	Is. 53:9	Mk. 15:43-46
Be raised from the dead	Ps. 16:10	Acts 2:22-32; Matt. 28:1-10
Sit at God's right hand	Ps. 110:1	Mk. 16:19; Lk. 24:50-51

All of these prophecies and more were fulfilled by one man: Jesus Christ. Could this have happened by chance? Let's look at the mathematical probability of one man fulfilling just eight of these prophecies:

1. **He would be born in Bethlehem.**
2. **He would have a forerunner.**
3. **He would enter Jerusalem on a donkey.**
4. **He would be betrayed by a friend.**
5. **He would be sold for silver.**
6. **The silver would be used to buy a field.**
7. **He would be silent before His accusers.**
8. **He would be pierced before death.**

In their book *Science Speaks*[19], Peter W. Stoner and Robert C. Newman, S.T.M., Ph.D[20] write that the probability of these eight prophecies being fulfilled by one man is 1 in 10^{17}.

In order to help us visualize this statistic, they write:

"Suppose that we take 10^{17} silver dollars and lay them on the face of Texas. They will cover all of the state two feet deep. Now mark one of these silver dollars and stir the whole mass thoroughly, all over the state. Blindfold a man and tell him that he can travel as far as he wishes, but he must pick up one silver dollar and say that this is the right one.

What chance would he have of getting the right one? Just the same chance that the prophets would have had of writing these eight prophecies and having them all come true in any one man, from their day to the present time, providing they wrote using their own wisdom. Now these prophecies were either given by inspiration of God or the prophets just wrote them as they thought they should be. In such a case the prophets had just one chance in 10^{17} of having them come true in any man, but they all came true in Christ.[21]"

Author's Note:

The preceeding statistics were carefully reviewed by a committee of American Scientific Affiliation members and by the Executive Council of the same group. In his foreword to the book *Science Speaks*, H. Harold Hartzler, Ph.D wrote on behalf of the committee:

> *"The mathematical analysis included is based upon principles of probability which are thoroughly sound and Professor Stoner has applied these principles in a proper and convincing way."*

---

[19] Stoner, Peter W., M.S. and Newman, Robert C.S.T.M., Ph.D.; *Science Speak,* Moody Press, Chicago, 1976, Chapter 3

[20] Peter Stoner, June 16, 1888 - March 21, 1980
PETER W. STONER, M.S.:
Chairman of the Departments of Mathematics and Astronomy at Pasadena City College until 1953; Chairman of the Science Division, Westmont College, 1953-57; Professor Emeritus of Science, Westmont College; Professor Emeritus of Mathematics and Astronomy, Pasadena City College.
ROBERT C. NEWMAN, S.T.M., Ph.D.:
Ph.D. in Astrophysics, Cornell University, 1967; S.T.M., Biblical School of Theology, 1972; Associate Professor of Physics and Mathematics, Shelton College, 1968-71; Associate professor of New Testament, Biblical School of Theology, 1971-

[21] http://sciencespeaks.dstoner.net/ Online edition to the book *Science Speaks*, prepared by Don W. Stoner, grandson of Peter W. Stoner

STUDY GUIDE APPENDIX

IS JESUS A MYTH?

Is Jesus just a copy of the pagan gods of other ancient religions?"

Answer: There are a number of people claiming that the accounts of Jesus as recorded in the New Testament are simply myths borrowed from pagan folklore, such as the stories of Osiris, Dionysus, Adonis, Attis, and Mithras. The claim is that these myths are essentially the same story as the New Testament's narrative of Jesus Christ of Nazareth. As Dan Brown claims in *The Da Vinci Code*, "Nothing in Christianity is original."

To discover the truth about the claim that the Gospel writers borrowed from mythology, it is important to (1) unearth the history behind the assertions, (2) examine the actual portrayals of the false gods being compared to Christ, (3) expose any logical fallacies being made, and (4) look at why the New Testament Gospels are trustworthy depictions of the true and historical Jesus Christ.

The claim that Jesus was a myth or an exaggeration originated in the writings of liberal German theologians in the nineteenth century. They essentially said that Jesus was nothing more than a copy of popular dying-and-rising fertility gods in various places—Tammuz in Mesopotamia, Adonis in Syria, Attis in Asia Minor, and Horus in Egypt. Of note is the fact that none of the books containing these theories were taken seriously by the academics of the day. The assertion that Jesus was a recycled Tammuz, for example, was investigated by contemporary scholars and determined to be completely baseless. It has only been recently that these assertions have been resurrected, primarily due to the rise of the Internet and the mass distribution of information from unaccountable sources.

This leads us to the next area of investigation—do the mythological gods of antiquity really mirror the person of Jesus Christ? As an example, the *Zeitgeist* movie makes these claims about the Egyptian god Horus:

- He was born on December 25 of a virgin: Isis Mary
- A star in the East proclaimed his arrival
- Three kings came to adore the newborn "savior"
- He became a child prodigy teacher at age 12
- At age 30 he was "baptized" and began a "ministry"
- Horus had twelve "disciples"
- Horus was betrayed
- He was crucified

- He was buried for three days
- He was resurrected after three days

However, when the actual writings about Horus are competently examined, this is what we find:

- Horus was born to Isis; there is no mention in history of her being called "Mary." Moreover, "Mary" is our Anglicized form of her real name, Miryam or Miriam. "Mary" was not even used in the original texts of Scripture.
- Isis was not a virgin; she was the widow of Osiris and conceived Horus with Osiris.
- Horus was born during month of Khoiak (Oct/Nov), not December 25. Further, there is no mention in the Bible as to Christ's actual birth date.
- There is no record of three kings visiting Horus at his birth. The Bible never states the actual number of magi that came to see Christ.
- Horus is not a "savior" in any way; he did not die for anyone.
- There are no accounts of Horus being a teacher at the age of 12.
- Horus was not "baptized." The only account of Horus that involves water is one story where Horus is torn to pieces, with Isis requesting the crocodile god to fish him out of the water.
- Horus did not have a "ministry."
- Horus did not have 12 disciples. According to the Horus accounts, Horus had four demigods that followed him, and there are some indications of 16 human followers and an unknown number of blacksmiths that went into battle with him.
- There is no account of Horus being betrayed by a friend.
- Horus did not die by crucifixion. There are various accounts of Horus' death, but none of them involve crucifixion.
- There is no account of Horus being buried for three days.
- Horus was not resurrected. There is no account of Horus coming out of the grave with the body he went in with. Some accounts have Horus/Osiris being brought back to life by Isis and then becoming the lord of the underworld.

When compared side by side, Jesus and Horus bear little, if any, resemblance to one another.

Jesus is also compared to Mithras by those claiming that Jesus Christ is a myth. All the above descriptions of Horus are applied to Mithras (e.g., born of a virgin, being crucified, rising in three days, etc.).

But what does the Mithras myth actually say?

- He was born out of a solid rock, not from any woman.
- He battled first with the sun and then with a primeval bull, thought to be the first act of creation. Mithras killed the bull, which then became the ground of life for the human race.
- Mithras's birth was celebrated on December 25, along with winter solstice.
- There is no mention of his being a great teacher.
- There is no mention of Mithras having 12 disciples. The idea that Mithras had 12 disciples may have come from a mural in which Mithras is surrounded by the twelve signs of the zodiac.
- Mithras had no bodily resurrection. Rather, when Mithras completed his earthly mission, he was taken to paradise in a chariot, alive and well. The early Christian writer Tertullian did write about Mithraic cultists re-enacting resurrection scenes, but this occurred well after New Testament times, so if any copycatting was done, it was Mithraism copying Christianity.

More examples can be given of Krishna, Attis, Dionysus, and other mythological gods, but the result is the same. In the end, the historical Jesus portrayed in the Bible is unique. The alleged similarities of Jesus' story to pagan myths are greatly exaggerated. Further, while tales of Horus, Mithras, and others pre-date Christianity, there is very little historical record of the *pre-Christian* beliefs of those religions. The vast majority of the earliest writings of these religions date from the third and fourth centuries A.D. To assume that the *pre*-Christian beliefs of these religions (of which there is no record) were identical to their *post*-Christian beliefs is naive. It is more logical to attribute any similarities between these religions and Christianity to the religions copying Christian teaching about Jesus.

This leads us to the next area to examine: the logical fallacies committed by those claiming that Christianity borrowed from pagan mystery religions. We'll consider two fallacies in particular: the fallacy of the false cause and the terminological fallacy.

If one thing precedes another, some conclude that the first thing must have caused the second. This is the fallacy of the false cause. A rooster may crow before the sunrise every morning, but that does not mean the rooster *causes* the sun to rise. Even if pre-Christian accounts of mythological gods closely resembled Christ (and they do not), it does not mean they caused the Gospel writers to invent a false Jesus. Making such a claim is akin to saying the TV series *Star Trek* caused the NASA Space Shuttle program.

The terminological fallacy occurs when words are redefined to prove a point. For example, the *Zeitgeist* movie says that Horus "began his ministry", but the word *ministry* is being redefined. Horus had no actual "ministry"—

nothing like that of Christ's ministry. Those claiming a link between Mithras and Jesus talk about the "baptism" that initiated prospects into the Mithras cult, but what was it actually? Mithraic priests would place initiates into a pit, suspend a bull over the pit, and slit the bull's stomach, covering the initiates in blood and gore. Such a practice bears no resemblance whatsoever to Christian baptism—a person going under water (symbolizing the death of Christ) and then coming back out of the water (symbolizing Christ's resurrection). But advocates of a mythological Jesus deceptively use the same term, "baptism", to describe both rites in hopes of linking the two.

This brings us to the subject of the truthfulness of the New Testament. No other work of antiquity has more evidence to its historical veracity than the New Testament. The New Testament has more writers (nine), better writers, and earlier writers than any other existing document from that era. Further, history testifies that these writers went to their deaths claiming that Jesus had risen from the dead. While some may die for a lie they think is true, no person dies for a lie he knows to be false. Think about it—if you were threatened with crucifixion, as tradition says happened to the apostle Peter, and all you had to do to save your life was renounce a lie you had knowingly told, what would you do?

In addition, history has shown that it takes at least two generations to pass before myth can enter a historical account. That's because as long as there are eyewitnesses to an event, errors can be refuted and mythical embellishments can be exposed. All the Gospels of the New Testament were written during the lifetime of the eyewitnesses, with some of Paul's Epistles being written as early as A.D. 50. Paul directly appeals to contemporary eyewitnesses to verify his testimony (1 Corinthians 15:6).

The New Testament attests to the fact that in the first century, Jesus was not mistaken for any other god. When Paul preached in Athens, the elite thinkers of that city said, "'He seems to be a proclaimer of strange deities,'—because he was preaching Jesus and the resurrection. And they took him and brought him to the Areopagus, saying, 'May we know what this new teaching is which you are proclaiming? For you are bringing some strange things to our ears; so we want to know what these things mean'" (Acts 17:18–20, NASB). Clearly, if Paul were simply rehashing stories of other gods, the Athenians would not have referred to his doctrine as a "new" and "strange" teaching. If dying-and-rising gods were plentiful in the first century, why, when the apostle Paul preached Jesus rising from the dead, did the Epicureans and Stoics not remark, "Ah, just like Horus and Mithras"?

In conclusion, the claim that Jesus is a copy of mythological gods originated with authors whose works have been discounted by academia, contain logical fallacies, and cannot compare to the New Testament Gospels, which have withstood nearly 2,000 years of intense scrutiny. The alleged parallels between Jesus and other gods disappear when the original myths are examined. The Jesus-is-a-myth theory relies on selective descriptions, redefined words, and false assumptions.

Jesus Christ is unique in history, with His voice rising above all false gods as He asks the question that ultimately determines a person's eternal destiny: "Who do you say I am?" (Matthew 16:15).

Recommended Resource: The Case for the Real Jesus by Lee Strobel

---

Used with Permission from GotQuestions

https://www.gotquestions.org/Jesus-myth.html

HOW DO WE KNOW JESUS EVER REALLY LIVED?

Q: *"Are there any historical writings, other than the Bible, that prove that Jesus ever really lived?"*

Our A: Yes. Cornelius Tacitus (A.D. 55-120) was considered the greatest historian of ancient Rome. He wrote of Nero who "punished with the most exquisite tortures, the persons commonly called Christians, who were hated for their enormities. Christus [Christ], the founder of the name, was put to death by Pontius Pilate, procurator of Judea in the reign of Tiberius: but the pernicious superstition, repressed for a time, broke out again, not only through Judea where the mischief originated, but through the city of Rome also."[1]

Also, Flavius Josephus, a Jewish historian, (A.D. 38-100+) wrote about Jesus in his *Jewish Antiquities,* saying that Jesus was a wise man who did surprising feats, taught many, won over followers from among Jews and Greeks, that Jesus was believed to be the Messiah, was accused by the Jewish leaders, was condemned to be crucified by Pilate, and was considered to be resurrected.[2]

The existence of Jesus Christ is recorded not only by Josephus and Tacitus, but also by ancient writers such as Suetonius, Thallus, Pliny the Younger, and Lucian. And from the Jewish *Talmud,* "we learn that Jesus was conceived out of wedlock, gathered disciples, made blasphemous claims about himself, and worked miracles, but these miracles are attributed to sorcery and not to God."[3]

Thus, historians both favorable and unfavorable regarding Jesus did write about him. Also there were many historical writings about the early Christians.
For more historical sources, please see https://www.everystudent.com/features/bible.html#4

Note: Many people also have an internal source of confirmation that Jesus existed, and still exists today.

The Bible says that God by His Spirit bears witness of Christ (John 15:26) and convinces the world concerning Him (John 16:8-11). So it's possible for someone without access to ancient historical writings or the Bible to believe that Jesus was real.

A person can hear about Jesus from another source, and God can confirm it by His Spirit.

Footnotes: (1) *Annals* XV, 44 as quoted in *The New Evidence That Demands a Verdict* by Josh McDowell. See this book for other historical sources. (2) Noted in *Jesus Under Fire* by Michael J. Wilkins and J. P. Moreland, Zondervan Publishing. (3) Ibid.

Used with Permission from EveryStudent

https://www.everystudent.com/forum/historical.html

DID JESUS REALLY EXIST?

Is there any historical evidence of Jesus Christ?

Answer: Typically, when this question is asked, the person asking qualifies the question with "outside of the Bible." We do not grant this idea that the Bible cannot be considered a source of evidence for the existence of Jesus. The New Testament contains hundreds of references to Jesus Christ. There are those who date the writing of the Gospels to the second century A.D., more than 100 years after Jesus' death. Even if this were the case (which we strongly dispute), in terms of ancient evidences, writings less than 200 years after events took place are considered very reliable evidences. Further, the vast majority of scholars (Christian and non-Christian) will grant that the Epistles of Paul (at least some of them) were in fact written by Paul in the middle of the first century A.D., less than 40 years after Jesus' death. In terms of ancient manuscript evidence, this is extraordinarily strong proof of the existence of a man named Jesus in Israel in the early first century A.D.

It is also important to recognize that in A.D. 70, the Romans invaded and destroyed Jerusalem and most of Israel, slaughtering its inhabitants. Entire cities were literally burned to the ground. We should not be surprised, then, if much evidence of Jesus' existence was destroyed. Many of the eyewitnesses of Jesus would have been killed. These facts likely limited the amount of surviving eyewitness testimony of Jesus.

Considering that Jesus' ministry was largely confined to a relatively unimportant area in a small corner of the Roman Empire, a surprising amount of information about Jesus can be drawn from secular historical sources. Some of the more important historical evidences of Jesus include the following:

The first-century Roman Tacitus, who is considered one of the more accurate historians of the ancient world, mentioned superstitious "Christians" (from Christus, which is Latin for Christ), who suffered under Pontius Pilate during the reign of Tiberius. Suetonius, chief secretary to Emperor Hadrian, wrote that there was a man named Chrestus (or Christ) who lived during the first century (Annals 15.44).

Flavius Josephus is the most famous Jewish historian. In his Antiquities he refers to James, "the brother of Jesus, who was called Christ." There is a controversial verse (18:3) that says, "Now there was about this time Jesus, a wise man, if it be lawful to call him a man. For he was one who wrought surprising feats....He was [the] Christ...he appeared to them alive again the third day, as the divine prophets had foretold these and ten thousand other wonderful things concerning him." One version reads, "At this time there was a wise man named Jesus. His conduct was good and [he] was known to be virtuous. And many people from among the Jews and the other nations became his disciples. Pilate condemned him to be crucified and to die. But those who became his disciples did not abandon his discipleship. They reported that He had appeared to them three days after his crucifixion, and that He was alive; accordingly He was perhaps the Messiah, concerning whom the prophets have recounted wonders."

Julius Africanus quotes the historian Thallus in a discussion of the darkness which followed the crucifixion of Christ (Extant Writings, 18).

Pliny the Younger, in Letters 10:96, recorded early Christian worship practices including the fact that Christians worshiped Jesus as God and were very ethical, and he includes a reference to the love feast and Lord's Supper.

The Babylonian Talmud (Sanhedrin 43a) confirms Jesus' crucifixion on the eve of Passover and the accusations against Christ of practicing sorcery and encouraging Jewish apostasy.

Lucian of Samosata was a second-century Greek writer who admits that Jesus was worshiped by Christians, introduced new teachings, and was crucified for them. He said that Jesus' teachings included the brotherhood of believers, the importance of conversion, and the importance of denying other gods. Christians lived according to Jesus' laws, believed themselves to be immortal, and were characterized by contempt for death, voluntary self-devotion, and renunciation of material goods.

Mara Bar-Serapion confirms that Jesus was thought to be a wise and virtuous man, was considered by many to be the king of Israel, was put to death by the Jews, and lived on in the teachings of His followers.

Then we have all the Gnostic writings (The Gospel of Truth, The Apocryphon of John, The Gospel of Thomas, The Treatise on Resurrection, etc.) that all mention Jesus.

In fact, we can almost reconstruct the gospel just from early non-Christian sources: Jesus was called the Christ (Josephus), did "magic", led Israel into new teachings, and was hanged on Passover for them (Babylonian Talmud) in Judea (Tacitus), but claimed to be God and would return (Eliezar), which his followers believed, worshipping Him as God (Pliny the Younger).

There is overwhelming evidence for the existence of Jesus Christ, both in secular and biblical history. Perhaps the greatest evidence that Jesus did exist is the fact that literally thousands of Christians in the first century A.D., including the twelve apostles, were willing to give their lives as martyrs for Jesus Christ. People will die for what they believe to be true, but no one will die for what they know to be a lie.

Recommended Resource: The Case for the Real Jesus by Lee Strobel

---

Used with Permission from GotQuestions

https://www.gotquestions.org/did-Jesus-exist.html

STUDY GUIDE APPENDIX

HOW CAN A LOVING GOD SEND PEOPLE TO HELL?

Q: "I'm trying to understand how God who is love can send people to be in hell. What's the thought behind going to hell?"

Our A: Here are some things to consider:

(1) God has given all people enough evidence to know that He exists.

"...What may be known about God is plain to them [people], because God has made it plain to them. For since the creation of the world God's invisible qualities – His eternal power and divine nature – have been clearly seen, being understood from what has been made, so that men are without excuse."[1]

"The heavens declare the glory of God; the skies proclaim the work of his hands."[2]

(2) Nonetheless, some people choose not to know Him.

"They exchanged the truth of God for a lie, and worshiped and served created things rather than the Creator."[3]

"The fool has said in his heart, 'there is no God.'"[4]

"We all, like sheep, have gone astray, each of us has turned to his own way."[5]

(3) People have been given free will. They can seek God and begin a relationship with Him, or reject God. Whatever people choose, their decision continues after they die.

Eternal life is life with God, eternally. And Jesus was clear that eternal life is gained by believing in Him. It is a relationship with God that is unending.

"For God so loved the world that He gave His one and only Son, that whoever believes in Him shall not perish but have eternal life."[6]

"Whoever believes in the Son has eternal life…"[7]

"I am the resurrection and the life. He who believes in me will live, even though he dies."[8]

God wants all people to know Him. However, the Bible also reveals that God does not force people to choose Him. He allows people to reject Him. God is love, but God allows people to reject His love, and to remain separated from Him. Jesus said, "*I tell you the truth, whoever hears My word and believes Him who sent Me has eternal life and will not be condemned; he has crossed over from death to life.*" [9]

Footnotes: (1) Romans 1:19,20 (2) Psalms 19:1 (3) Romans 1:25 (4) Psalms 14:1 (5) Isaiah 53:6 (6) John 3:16 (7) John 3:36 (8) John 11:25 (9) John 5:24

Used with Permission from EveryStudent

https://www.everystudent.com/forum/punish.html

STUDY GUIDE APPENDIX

WHAT HAPPENS THEN?

Life now. Life then. Life after death?

Today maybe you're in college. Somewhere between the ages of 18 and 24. But what about Tomorrow?

You graduate. You get a job. You get married. You have children. You go through a few more jobs. You buy a house. Okay, THEN what?

You go to soccer games for your kids. You try to be a good parent and spouse. You watch your children go to the prom even though yesterday they were wearing diapers. You do and say the things your parents did and said, even though you vowed you never would.

You have a mid-life crisis or two. Your children graduate from college. You become a grandparent. Someone calls you grandma or grandpa. You live out your life in leisure, drawing income from a retirement fund. You take walks in the morning. You work in the garden. You read the newspaper.

You watch TV. You talk to your children and grandchildren on the phone. You travel.
Okay, THEN what?

Well, then someday you die. If you are fortunate, you live a relatively long life. Seventy to 90 years. If you don't get taken away prematurely by cancer or a car accident. But always, eventually, you die.

Death is the Tomorrow that awaits us all, the inevitable *Then* that none of us can escape.
But is that it? Is there anything more?

Someday you'll be just a corpse. They'll bury your body in the ground. Or burn your body and put your ashes in an urn. The big question is, *Will I cease after that? Will there still be a conscious ME somewhere? Is there really life after death?*

In truth, we probably all hope there is something that comes after. Maybe in the smallest recesses of our minds, we are planning on it.

What are we planning on? A life after death of some sort. Some call it paradise. Some call it heaven. Some also talk of hell.

Another thought that many people possess throughout life, often subconsciously, is: *I'm a basically good person. Therefore, I will get to go to heaven someday.*

Is that how it works?

Many people think they are "good enough" for heaven. It's an assumption we make. If we haven't robbed a bank, or murdered anyone, or cheated on our taxes, we think we're just the kind of folk God is looking for to populate His home. By golly, we are good enough.

At heaven's box office, we bought our ticket by being basically good people all throughout our lives. But what if that thinking is incorrect? THEN what? What a thing to have been wrong about! What a misfire!

If you think you're good enough for heaven, there are two things to consider:

(1) If heaven is a place of perfection[1], how can *anyone* be good enough?

Most of us would say we have a "skeleton in the closet." At least one. Something we hope no one ever finds out about us. A mistake in our past. A poor decision. A moment of weakness or stupidity that we'd rather not think about.

That's the extreme. But there are many other more common things we don't really want others to know or notice about us. It might be the "little white lies" we tell. Or how we talk behind someone's back. Or how we copy other people's homework. Or the unkind words we say to people. Or the unkind thoughts we have about people.

Much more than a one-time regrettable event, our lives, if we closely scrutinize them, show a pattern of wrongdoing. We often don't do what we believe to be right. And we often do what we believe is wrong.

All of us, even people whom we would call basically good, are also basically selfish and basically very imperfect.[2] Everything we do is seen by God.[3] So that means there's no fooling Him. He's perfectly aware of all the good we haven't done (and yet could have), as well as all the bad we've done. He even knows all of our thoughts and all of our motives.

Here's the second thing to consider if we think we're "good enough" for heaven:

(2) Is it possible to be a basically good person and still have rejected God?

Consider Ralph. He's a "good" person. He was ethical in his job. He never stole even a paper clip. He was a faithful father and husband. He provided for his children. He made sacrifices for them and for his wife (whom he never cheated on). He even gave money to many charities throughout his life.

But Ralph, though good in some sense, never "let God in". Many times in his life, Ralph sensed God's desire to come into his life. It was as if God were knocking on the door of Ralph's heart. But Ralph never opened that door. He always came up with some excuse not to. Ironically, one of the recurring excuses was, *I've been a good person all my life. I will go to heaven.*

Ralph wanted to go to heaven. Everyone does. But in reality, Ralph didn't want to know God. And he didn't stop to analyze the huge implications of that decision (the decision to keep God out).

Think about it. Heaven is God's home. If Ralph didn't want to know God during his life on Earth, why would Ralph want to know God in an afterlife? In other words, what Ralph didn't calculate is how much he would LOATHE heaven.

Heaven is a place where God is very present. It's likely that every aspect of heaven will remind one of God, constantly. What a horrible place for Ralph!

Ralph always assumed heaven would be a place of ultimate comfort. But he never considered how ultimately uncomfortable it would be for him, since he didn't want to know God or have a relationship with God. For Ralph, heaven would not be heaven, but rather a type of hell.

Would you let someone into your home even if you knew they didn't want to have anything to do with you? If you knew that everywhere they turned, they'd be reminded of you?

Many people are like Ralph. They want heaven, but they don't want God. And they don't realize that, under those circumstances, heaven would be an awful place to be.

WHAT HAPPENS THEN?

Maybe the truth of the matter is that heaven is for people who know they're not good enough to be there -- but who nonetheless want to be there solely because God is there. They want to know God and be with Him forever. The life-after-death prize isn't heaven, but rather its Primary Occupant.

Do you want to know God? Do you want to learn how to become "good enough" for heaven? See Knowing God Personally.[22]

Go to the link in the footnotes to watch "Bulletproof Faith[23]"

Footnotes: (1) *"Nothing impure will ever enter it, nor will anyone who does what is shameful or deceitful."* (Revelation 21:27)
(2) *"No one is good – except God alone."* (Luke 18:19); more: Isaiah 53:6, Romans 3:10, Romans 3:23, James 2:10
(3) *"Nothing in all creation is hidden from God's sight. Everything is uncovered and laid bare before the eyes of him to whom we must give account."* (Hebrews 4:13); more: Matthew 10:26, 1 Corinthians 4:5

Used with Permission from EveryStudent

https://www.everystudent.com/journeys/then.html

---

[22] https://www.everystudent.com/features/gettingconnected.html

[23] https://www.everystudent.com/videos/bpfaith.html - BulletProof Faith

STUDY GUIDE APPENDIX

WHY DID JESUS DIE?

The crucifixion of Jesus is a highly significant event for those who believe in Jesus. Here's what happened.

The religious leaders in Jerusalem arrested Jesus, charging Him with blasphemy for claiming to be God. They brought Jesus before the occupying Roman government for sentencing. Pilate, who had the final say, believed Jesus should be set free. But the crowds demanded that Jesus be put to death. "Crucify him! Crucify him!" The verdict: death by crucifixion, the Roman government's method of torture and death.

None of this was a surprise to Jesus. Many times, prior to His crucifixion, Jesus told His disciples that He was going to be arrested, beaten, crucified. He also said that three days after being buried he would come back to life. Jesus said He was laying down his life willingly, for the forgiveness of our sins.

However, the religious leaders were correct. Jesus was very clear about His deity. Jesus said He existed before the creation of the world,[1] that He had power to forgive sins,[2] and answer prayer[3] and grant eternal life.[4] He said to know Him was to know God.[5] To see Him was to see God.[6] To believe in Him was to believe in God.[7] To receive Him was to receive God.[8] To hate Him was to hate God.[9] And to honor Him was to honor God.[10] Jesus offered convincing proof for these statements.

Before Jesus' Crucifixion

For example, only weeks before His crucifixion, a close friend of Jesus' named Lazarus died. Jesus was in another town at the time, but mutual friends sent word to him. By the time Jesus arrived, Lazarus had been buried for four days. Jesus brought him back to life. There were many witnesses, and news spread quickly.

In town after town, Jesus healed every disease, every sickness. He fed crowds of 4,000 people who came to hear Him preach. Another time, 5,000 people. The religious authorities complained, "Look, the world has gone after Him,"[11] "If we let Him go on like this, everyone will believe in Him..."[12]

Jesus' death on the cross was not merely the natural consequences of His miracles and His statements. He was not at their mercy.

Jesus had already proved He had absolute power. In light of that, the whipping, thorns in His head, nails through His wrists and feet did not kill Him. Neither did the slow suffocation on the cross. Jesus could have stepped off the cross at any moment. This was the equivalent of someone bending over and putting their head under water, and choosing to deliberately drown when they had the power to raise their head at any moment. Jesus chose to die. Jesus said, "No one takes My life from Me. I lay it down of my own choosing."[13] He did so purposefully. It was planned. Intentional.

And here's why...

Why Did Jesus Die

To varying degrees, we act in ways that are opposed to God's ways. Just take a quick scan of the news on any given day…racism, murders, sexual abuse, lies, greed, corruption, terrorism, wars, etc. As people we have a great way of messing up our lives and the lives of others. God sees us as lost, blind and under His judgment for our ways. Think how sickened and grieved we are to hear that a 6-year-old girl is kidnapped from her family for sexual abuse. It's such an affront to our moral senses, that even those who oppose the death penalty might be tempted.

Well, *all* of our sin is an affront to a holy God. All of our sin grieves Him. We don't live up to our own standards, let alone His. When honest, we even disgust ourselves at times. So what would a perfectly holy God see?

God says that the penalty for sin is death.[14] This is why, in the Old Testament you see God instructing the Israelites to sacrifice a lamb once a year for the forgiveness of their sins. The lamb died in their place. But that was a temporary forgiveness. They had to do this each year. When Jesus came, the prophet John the Baptist said this about Jesus, "Behold, the lamb of God who takes away the sins of the world."[15]

Jesus came to take the penalty for humanity's sin, for our sin, in our place. Rather than us die and be permanently, eternally separated from God, Jesus paid for our sin on the cross, in order that we could be forever forgiven and have eternal life. This is exactly why Jesus came, as our Savior, to save us from God's judgment, condemnation and payment of our sin. Any sin you have ever committed, or will do, Jesus was aware of while hanging on the cross. Jesus took the punishment for our sins for us.

DaVinci's Last Supper

You've seen the famous painting by Leonardo da Vinci of the "Last Supper" with Jesus sitting at a long table and the disciples sitting next to him on both sides of him. Da Vinci was depicting the dinner that Jesus had with his disciples the night before he was arrested and crucified. At that "Last Supper" Jesus told His disciples that His blood would be "poured out for many for the forgiveness of sins."[16]

Jesus was beaten, whipped nearly to death with a metal or bone tipped "cat-o-nine-tails" torture device, then his wrists and feet nailed to a cross, then uprighted, where He hung until death. A spear was thrust into His side to confirm His death. Jesus, who knew no sin, paid for our sin on the cross. It's not fair. We didn't deserve for Him to take our place. Why would He do it?

We're told, "God shows His love toward us in this: while we were yet sinners, Christ died for us."[17]

Our Response to the Crucifixion of Jesus

What does he ask of us? To earn our forgiveness? No. We could never be worthy of what Jesus did for us. What He asks of us is simple…to believe in Him. He asks us to accept His death on our behalf, to accept His complete forgiveness as a free gift.

Oddly enough, many people don't want to do this. They want to try to earn their own salvation. Earn their own way into heaven. They want to show by their efforts that they are worthy of a relationship with God. Jesus said they will die in their sin and face judgment, because they reject what Jesus did for them. The disciple Peter said of Jesus, "everyone who believes in Him receives forgiveness of sins through His name."[18]

But not only forgiveness, also eternal life and a close, personal relationship with God now, in this life. It is all ours, because Jesus died on the cross for us. Jesus was not merely taking punishment for our sin. He was eliminating the wall that stood between us and God. He was offering far more than forgiveness. He was offering reconciliation, full acceptance, a full relationship with Him, so we could know His love for us.
This is like a wealthy billionaire not only cancelling the debt a person owes him, but then turning over his entire estate to the person who couldn't pay him back.

Eternal life, heaven, is a free gift: "For the payment for sin is death, but the gift of God is eternal life in Christ Jesus our Lord."[19]

Jesus came into the world to die for us, to provide a way for us to know Him intimately. It is our decision to receive the gift of a relationship with Him that He is offering us. Jesus summarized it this way, "I am the way, the truth, and the life; no one comes to the Father except through Me."[20]

His Offer to Us

Anyone who will invite Jesus into their lives and accept his free gift of forgiveness and eternal life, begins a never-ending relationship with Him.

After His crucifixion, they buried Jesus in a tomb and stationed a trained Roman guard of soldiers at His tomb. Why? Jesus had repeatedly said that three days after His burial, He would rise from the dead. It would prove everything He said about Himself. Three days later, the tomb was empty. Jesus then physically appeared to the disciples many times, to a crowd of 500, to individuals. Each of Jesus' disciples went throughout the world proclaiming Jesus' resurrection. Each one was martyred for it, in different locations from each other, so convinced of Jesus' identity.

It is our decision whether to accept the forgiveness He offers, by moving toward Him, asking Him to forgive us and enter our lives. John states it well in the Bible, "We have come to know and to believe the love that God has for us. God is love, and whoever abides in love abides in God, and God abides in him. By this is love perfected with us, so that we may have confidence for the day of judgment."[21]

Jesus explicitly stated, "Truly, truly, I say to you, whoever hears my word and believes Him who sent Me has eternal life. He does not come into judgment, but has passed from death to life."[22]

Jesus' prayer right before His death: "Righteous Father, though the world does not know you, I know you, and they [Jesus' followers] know that you have sent me. I have made you known to them, and will continue to make you known in order that the love you have for me may be in them and that I myself may be in them."[23]
Would you like to invite Jesus Christ into your life right now? Here is how you can.

"Jesus, I ask you to come into my life. Forgive my sin. Thank you for dying on the cross for me. Lead my life as you want. Thank you for coming into my life right now and giving me a relationship with you. Amen."

Footnotes: (1) John 17:24 (2) Matthew 9:6 (3) John 14:13,14 (4) John 5:24 (5) John 8:19 (6) John 12:45; 14:9 (7) John 12:44; 14:1 (8) Mark 9:37 (9) John 15:23 (10) John 5:23 (11) John 12:19 (12) John 11:48 (13) John 10:18 (14) Romans 6:23 (15) John 1:29 (16) Matthew 26:28 (17) Romans 5:8 (18) Acts 10:43 (19) Romans 6:23 (20) John 14:6 (21) 1John 4:16,17 (22) John 5:24 (23) John 17:25,26

Used with Permission from EveryStudent

https://www.everystudent.com/wires/whydid.html

STUDY GUIDE APPENDIX

"WHY SHOULD I BELIEVE IN CHRIST'S RESURRECTION?"

Answer: It is a fairly well-established fact that Jesus Christ was publicly executed in Judea in the 1st Century A.D., under Pontius Pilate, by means of crucifixion, at the behest of the Jewish Sanhedrin. The non-Christian historical accounts of Flavius Josephus, Cornelius Tacitus, Lucian of Samosata, Maimonides and even the Jewish Sanhedrin corroborate the early Christian eyewitness accounts of these important historical aspects of the death of Jesus Christ.

As for His resurrection, there are several lines of evidence which make for a compelling case. The late jurisprudential prodigy and international statesman Sir Lionel Luckhoo (of The Guinness Book of World Records fame for his unprecedented 245 consecutive defense murder trial acquittals) epitomized Christian enthusiasm and confidence in the strength of the case for the resurrection when he wrote, "I have spent more than 42 years as a defense trial lawyer appearing in many parts of the world and am still in active practice. I have been fortunate to secure a number of successes in jury trials and I say unequivocally the evidence for the Resurrection of Jesus Christ is so overwhelming that it compels acceptance by proof which leaves absolutely no room for doubt."

The secular community's response to the same evidence has been predictably apathetic in accordance with their steadfast commitment to methodological naturalism. For those unfamiliar with the term, methodological naturalism is the human endeavor of explaining everything in terms of natural causes and natural causes only. If an alleged historical event defies natural explanation (e.g., a miraculous resurrection), secular scholars generally treat it with overwhelming skepticism, regardless of the evidence, no matter how favorable and compelling it may be.

In our view, such an unwavering allegiance to natural causes regardless of substantive evidence to the contrary is not conducive to an impartial (and therefore adequate) investigation of the evidence. We agree with Dr. Wernher von Braun and numerous others who still believe that forcing a popular philosophical predisposition upon the evidence hinders objectivity. Or in the words of Dr. von Braun, "To be forced to believe only one conclusion… would violate the very objectivity of science itself."

Having said that, let us now examine several lines of evidence for Christ's resurrection.

The First Line of Evidence for Christ's resurrection

To begin with, we have demonstrably sincere eyewitness testimony. Early Christian apologists cited hundreds of eyewitnesses, some of whom documented their own alleged experiences. Many of these eyewitnesses willfully and resolutely endured prolonged torture and death rather than repudiate their testimony. This fact attests to their sincerity, ruling out deception on their part. According to the historical record (The Book of Acts 4:1-17; Pliny's Letters to Trajan X, 97, etc) most Christians could end their suffering simply by renouncing the faith. Instead, it seems that most opted to endure the suffering and proclaim Christ's resurrection unto death.

Granted, while martyrdom is remarkable, it is not necessarily compelling. It does not validate a belief so much as it authenticates a believer (by demonstrating his or her sincerity in a tangible way). What makes the earliest Christian martyrs remarkable is that they knew whether or not what they were professing was true. They either saw Jesus Christ alive-and-well after His death or they did not. This is extraordinary. If it was all just a lie, why would so many perpetuate it given their circumstances? Why would they all knowingly cling to such an unprofitable lie in the face of persecution, imprisonment, torture, and death?

While the September 11, 2001, suicide hijackers undoubtedly believed what they professed (as evidenced by their willingness to die for it), they could not and did not know if it was true. They put their faith in traditions passed down to them over many generations. In contrast, the early Christian martyrs were the first generation. Either they saw what they claimed to see, or they did not.

Among the most illustrious of the professed eyewitnesses were the Apostles. They collectively underwent an undeniable change following the alleged post-resurrection appearances of Christ. Immediately following His crucifixion, they hid in fear for their lives. Following the resurrection they took to the streets, boldly proclaiming the resurrection despite intensifying persecution. What accounts for their sudden and dramatic change? It certainly was not financial gain. The Apostles gave up everything they had to preach the resurrection, including their lives.

The Second Line of Evidence for Christ's resurrection

A second line of evidence concerns the conversion of certain key skeptics, most notably Paul and James. Paul was of his own admission a violent persecutor of the early Church. After what he described as an encounter with the resurrected Christ, Paul underwent an immediate and drastic change from a vicious persecutor of the Church to one of its most prolific and selfless defenders. Like many early Christians, Paul suffered impoverishment, persecution, beatings, imprisonment, and execution for his steadfast commitment to Christ's resurrection.

James was skeptical, though not as hostile as Paul. A purported post-resurrection encounter with Christ turned him into an inimitable believer, a leader of the Church in Jerusalem. We still have what scholars generally accept to be one of his letters to the early Church. Like Paul, James willingly suffered and died for his testimony, a fact which attests to the sincerity of his belief (see The Book of Acts and Josephus' Antiquities of the Jews XX, ix, 1).

The Third and Fourth Lines of Evidence for Christ's resurrection

A third line and fourth line of evidence concern enemy attestation to the empty tomb and the fact that faith in the resurrection took root in Jerusalem. Jesus was publicly executed and buried in Jerusalem. It would have been impossible for faith in His resurrection to take root in Jerusalem while His body was still in the tomb where the Sanhedrin could exhume it, put it on public display, and thereby expose the hoax. Instead, the Sanhedrin accused the disciples of stealing the body, apparently in an effort to explain its disappearance (and therefore an empty tomb). How do we explain the fact of the empty tomb? Here are the three most common explanations:

First, the disciples stole the body. If this were the case, they would have known the resurrection was a hoax. They would not therefore have been so willing to suffer and die for it. (See the first line of evidence concerning demonstrably sincere eyewitness testimony.) All of the professed eyewitnesses would have known that they hadn't really seen Christ and were therefore lying. With so many conspirators, surely someone would have confessed, if not to end his own suffering then at least to end the suffering of his friends and family. The first generation of Christians were absolutely brutalized, especially following the conflagration in Rome in A.D. 64 (a fire which Nero allegedly ordered to make room for the expansion of his palace, but which he blamed on the Christians in Rome in an effort to exculpate himself). As the Roman historian Cornelius Tacitus recounted in his Annals of Imperial Rome (published just a generation after the fire):

"Nero fastened the guilt and inflicted the most exquisite tortures on a class hated for their abominations, called Christians by the populace. Christus, from whom the name had its origin, suffered the extreme penalty during the reign of Tiberius at the hands of one of our procurators, Pontius Pilatus, and a most mischievous superstition, thus checked for the moment, again broke out not only in Judaea, the first source of the evil, but even in Rome, where all things hideous and shameful from every part of the world find their centre and become popular. Accordingly, an arrest was first made of all who pleaded guilty; then, upon their information, an immense multitude was convicted, not so much of the crime of firing the city, as of hatred against mankind. Mockery of every sort was added to their deaths. Covered with the skins of beasts, they were torn by dogs and perished, or were nailed to crosses, or were doomed to the flames and burnt, to serve as a nightly illumination, when daylight had expired." (Annals, XV, 44)

Nero illuminated his garden parties with Christians whom he burnt alive. Surely someone would have confessed the truth under the threat of such terrible pain. The fact is, however, we have no record of any early Christian denouncing the faith to end his suffering. Instead, we have multiple accounts of post-resurrection appearances and hundreds of eyewitnesses willing to suffer and die for it.

If the disciples didn't steal the body, how else do we explain the empty tomb? Some have suggested that Christ faked His death and later escaped from the tomb. This is patently absurd. According to the eyewitness testimony, Christ was beaten, tortured, lacerated, and stabbed. He suffered internal damage, massive blood loss, asphyxiation, and a spear through His heart. There is no good reason to believe that Jesus Christ (or any other man for that matter) could survive such an ordeal, fake His death, sit in a tomb for three days and nights without medical attention, food or water, remove the massive stone which sealed His tomb, escape undetected (without leaving behind a trail of blood), convince hundreds of eyewitnesses that He was resurrected from the death and in good health, and then disappear without a trace. Such a notion is ridiculous.

The Fifth Line of Evidence for Christ's resurrection

Finally, a fifth line of evidence concerns a peculiarity of the eyewitness testimony. In all of the major resurrection narratives, women are credited as the first and primary eyewitnesses. This would be an odd invention since in both the ancient Jewish and Roman cultures women were severely disesteemed. Their testimony was regarded as insubstantial and dismissible. Given this fact, it is highly unlikely that any perpetrators of a hoax in 1st Century Judea would elect women to be their primary witnesses. Of all the male disciples who claimed to see Jesus resurrected, if they all were lying and the resurrection was a scam, why did they pick the most ill-perceived, distrusted witnesses they could find?

Dr. William Lane Craig explains, "When you understand the role of women in first-century Jewish society, what's really extraordinary is that this empty tomb story should feature women as the discoverers of the empty tomb in the first place. Women were on a very low rung of the social ladder in first-century Israel. There are old rabbinical sayings that said, 'Let the words of Law be burned rather than delivered to women' and 'blessed is he whose children are male, but woe to him whose children are female.' Women's testimony was regarded as so worthless that they weren't even allowed to serve as legal witnesses in a Jewish court of law. In light of this, it's absolutely remarkable that the chief witnesses to the empty tomb are these women...Any later legendary account would have certainly portrayed male disciples as discovering the tomb - Peter or John, for example. The fact that women are the first witnesses to the empty tomb is most plausibly explained by the reality that - like it or not - they were the discoverers of the empty tomb! This shows that the Gospel writers faithfully recorded what happened, even if it was embarrassing. This bespeaks the historicity of this tradition rather than its legendary status." (Dr. William Lane Craig, quoted by Lee Strobel, The Case For Christ, Grand Rapids: Zondervan, 1998, p. 293)

In Summary

These lines of evidence: the demonstrable sincerity of the eyewitnesses (and in the Apostles' case, compelling, inexplicable change), the conversion and demonstrable sincerity of key antagonists- and skeptics-turned-martyrs, the fact of the empty tomb, enemy attestation to the empty tomb, the fact that all of this took place in Jerusalem where faith in the resurrection began and thrived, the testimony of the women, the significance of such testimony given the historical context; all of these strongly attest to the historicity of the resurrection. We encourage our readers to thoughtfully consider these evidences. What do they suggest to you? Having pondered them ourselves, we resolutely affirm Sir Lionel's declaration:

"The evidence for the Resurrection of Jesus Christ is so overwhelming that it compels acceptance by proof which leaves absolutely no room for doubt."

Recommended Resource: The Case for the Resurrection of Jesus by Gary Habermas

---

Used with Permission from GotQuestions
https://www.gotquestions.org/why-believe-resurrection.html

BEYOND BLIND FAITH

Who is Jesus? Is Jesus God? See what Jesus said about Himself, His equality with God, and what exactly Jesus did to prove it.

By Paul E. Little

It is impossible for us to know conclusively whether God exists and what He is like unless He takes the initiative and reveals Himself.

We must scan the horizon of history to see if there is any clue to God's revelation. There is one clear clue. In an obscure village in Palestine, 2,000 years ago, a Child was born in a stable. Today the entire world is still celebrating the birth of Jesus, and for good reason.

Did Jesus ever claim to be God?

We're told that "the common people heard him gladly." And, "He taught as One who had authority, and not as their teachers of the Law."[1]

It soon became apparent, however, that He was making shocking and startling statements about Himself. He began to identify Himself as far more than a remarkable teacher or prophet. He began to say clearly that He was God. He made his identity the focal point of His teaching. The all-important question he put to those who followed Him was, "Who do you say I am?" When Peter answered and said, "You are the Christ, the Son of the living God,"[2] Jesus was not shocked, nor did He rebuke Peter. On the contrary, He commended him!

Jesus frequently referred to "My Father", and His hearers got the full impact of his words. We are told, "The Jews tried all the harder to kill Him; not only was He breaking the Sabbath, but He was even calling God His own Father, making Himself equal with God."[3]

On another occasion He said, "I and My Father are One." Immediately the religious authorities wanted to stone Him. He asked them which of His good works caused them to want to kill Him. They replied, "We are not stoning you for any of these but for blasphemy, because you, a mere man, claim to be God."[4]

Look at His life.

As Jesus was healing a paralyzed man, Jesus said to him, "Son, your sins are forgiven you." The religious leaders immediately reacted. "Why does this fellow talk like that? He's blaspheming! Who can forgive sins but God alone?"

When Jesus was on trial for His life, the high priest put the question to Him directly: "Are you the Christ, the Son of the Blessed One?" "I am", said Jesus. "And you will see the Son of Man sitting at the right hand of the Mighty One and coming on the clouds of heaven." The high priest rendered the verdict. "Why do we need any more witnesses?" he asked. "You have heard His blasphemy."[5]

So close was Jesus' connection with God that He equated a person's attitude to himself with the person's attitude toward God. Thus, to know Him was to know God.[6] To see Him was to see God.[7] To believe in Him was to believe in God.[8] To receive Him was to receive God.[9] To hate Him was to hate God.[10] And to honor Him was to honor God.[11]

Possible explanations

"As we face the claims of Christ, there are only four possibilities. He was either a liar, mentally ill, a legend, or the Truth."

The question is, was He telling the truth?

Maybe Jesus lied when He said He was God. Perhaps He knew He was not God, but deliberately deceived His hearers. But there is a problem with this reasoning. Even those who deny His deity affirm that He was a great moral teacher. Jesus could hardly be a great moral teacher if, on the most crucial point of his teaching -- His identity -- He was a deliberate liar.

Another possibility is that Jesus was sincere but self-deceived. We have a name for a person today who thinks he is God. Mentally disabled. But as we look at the life of Christ, we see no evidence of the abnormality and imbalance we find in a mentally ill person. Rather, we find the greatest composure under pressure.

A third alternative is that His enthusiastic followers put words into His mouth He would have been shocked to hear. Were He to return, He would immediately repudiate them.

No, modern archeology verifies that four biographies of Christ were written within the lifetime of people who saw, heard and followed Jesus. These gospel accounts contained specific facts and descriptions confirmed by those who were eyewitnesses of Jesus. The early writing of the Gospels by Matthew, Mark, Luke and John, is why they gained such circulation and impact, unlike the fictional Gnostic gospels which appeared centuries later.

Jesus was not a liar, or mentally disabled, or manufactured apart from historical reality. The only other alternative is that Jesus was being consciously truthful when He said He was God.

What is the proof?

From one point of view, however, claims don't mean much. Talk is cheap. Anyone can make claims. There have been others who have claimed to be God. I could claim to be God, and you could claim to be God, but the question all of us must answer is, "What credentials do we bring to substantiate our claim?" In my case it wouldn't take you five minutes to disprove my claim. It probably wouldn't take too much more to dispose of yours.

But when it comes to Jesus of Nazareth, it's not so simple. He had the credentials to back up His claim. He said, "Even though you do not believe Me, believe the evidence of the miracles, that you may learn and understand that the Father is in Me, and I am in the Father."[12]

The life of Jesus - His unique moral character

His moral character coincided with His claims. The quality of His life was such that He was able to challenge His very enemies with the question, "Can any of you prove Me guilty of sin?"[13] He was met by silence, even though He addressed those who would have liked to point out a flaw in His character.

We read of Jesus being tempted by Satan, but we never hear of a confession of sin on His part. He never asked for forgiveness, though He told his followers to do so.

This lack of any sense of moral failure on Jesus' part is astonishing in view of the fact that it is completely contrary to the experience of the saints and mystics throughout the ages. The closer men and women draw to God, the more overwhelmed they are with their own failure, corruption, and shortcomings. The closer one is to a shining light, the more he realizes his need of a bath. This is true also, in the moral realm, for ordinary mortals.

It is also striking that John, Paul, and Peter, all of whom were trained from earliest childhood to believe in the universality of sin, all spoke of the sinlessness of Christ: "He committed no sin, and no deceit was found in His mouth."[14]

Even Pilate, who sentenced Jesus to death, asked, "What evil has He done?" After listening to the crowd, Pilate concluded, "I am innocent of this man's blood; see to it yourselves." The crowd relentlessly demanded Jesus be crucified (for blasphemy, claiming to be God). The Roman centurion who assisted in the crucifixion of Christ said, "Surely He was the Son of God."[15]

He cured the sick

Jesus constantly demonstrated His power and compassion. He made the lame to walk, the blind to see, and healed those with diseases. For example, a man who had been blind from birth. Everyone knew him as the familiar beggar who sat outside the temple. Yet Jesus healed him. As the authorities questioned the beggar about Jesus, he said, "One thing I do know. I was blind but now I see!" he declared. He was astounded that these religious authorities didn't recognize this Healer as the Son of God. "Nobody has ever heard of opening the eyes of a man born blind," he said.[16] To him the evidence was obvious.

His ability to control nature

Jesus also demonstrated a supernatural power over nature itself. He commanded a raging storm of high wind and waves on the Sea of Galilee to be calm. Those in the boat were awestruck, asking, "Who is this? Even the wind and waves obey Him!"[17] He turned water into wine, at a wedding. He fed a massive crowd of 5,000 people, starting with five loaves of bread and two fish. He gave a grieving widow back her only son by raising him from the dead.

Lazarus, a friend of Jesus', died and was buried in a tomb for four days already. Yet Jesus said, "Lazarus, come forth!" and dramatically raised him from the dead, witnessed by many. It is most significant that His enemies did not deny this miracle. Rather, they decided to kill Him. "If we let Him go on like this," they said, "everyone will believe in Him."[18]

Is Jesus God, as he claimed?

Jesus' supreme evidence of deity was His own resurrection from the dead. Five times in the course of His life, Jesus clearly predicted in what specific way He would be killed and affirmed that three days later he would rise from the dead.

Surely this was the great test. It was a claim that was easy to verify. It would either happen or not. It would either confirm His stated identity or destroy it. And significant for you and me, Jesus' rising from the dead would verify or make laughable statements such as these:

"I am the way, the truth, and the life; no one comes to the Father except through Me."[19] "I am the light of the world. He who follows Me will not live in darkness, but will have the light of life."[20] For those who believe in Him, "I give them eternal life..."[21]

So by his own words, He offers this proof, ""The Son of Man is going to be delivered into the hands of men, and they will kill Him. And when He is killed, after three days He will rise."[22]

What this would mean

> "Talk is cheap. Anyone can make claims. But when it comes to Jesus of Nazareth... He had the credentials to back up His claim."

If Christ rose, we know with certainty that God exists, what God is like, and how we may know Him in personal experience. The universe takes on meaning and purpose, and it is possible to experience the living God in this life.

On the other hand, if Christ did not rise from the dead, Christianity has no objective validity or reality. The martyrs who went singing to the lions, and contemporary missionaries who have given their lives while taking this message to others, have been poor deluded fools. Paul, the great apostle, wrote, "If Christ has not been raised, our preaching is useless and so is your faith."[23] Paul rested his whole case on the bodily resurrection of Christ.

Did Jesus prove He is God?

Let's look at the evidence for Jesus' resurrection.

Given all the miracles He had performed, Jesus easily could have avoided the cross, but He chose not to. Before His arrest, Jesus said, "I lay down my life that I may take it up again. No one takes it from Me, but I lay it down of my own accord...and I have authority to take it up again."[24]

During his arrest, Jesus' friend Peter tried to defend Him. But Jesus said to Peter, "Put your sword back into its place...Do you think that I cannot appeal to my Father, and He will at once send Me more than twelve legions of angels?"[25] He had that kind of power in heaven and on earth. Jesus went willingly to His death.

Jesus' crucifixion and burial.

Jesus' death was by public execution on a cross, a common form of torture and death, used by the Roman government for many centuries. The accusation against Jesus was for blasphemy (for claiming to be God). Jesus said it was to pay for our sin.

Jesus was lashed with a multi-cord whip having metal or bone fragmented ends. A mock crown of long thorns was beaten into His skull. They forced Him to walk to an execution hill outside of Jerusalem. They put Him on a wooden cross, nailing His wrists and feet to it. He hung there, eventually dying. A sword was thrust into His side to confirm His death.

The body of Jesus was taken from the cross, wrapped in mummy-like linens covered with gummy-wet spices. His body was placed in a solid rock tomb, where a very large boulder was rolled down to it, to secure the entrance.

Everyone knew that Jesus said He would rise from the dead in three days. So they stationed a guard of trained Roman soldiers at the tomb. They also affixed an official Roman seal to the outside of the tomb declaring it government property.

Three days later, the tomb was empty.

In spite of all this, three days later the boulder, formerly sealing the tomb, was found up a slope, some distance away from the tomb. The body was gone. Only the grave linens were found in the tomb, caved in, empty of the body.

It is important to note that both critics and followers of Jesus agree that the tomb was empty and the body missing. The earliest explanation circulated was that the disciples stole the body while the guards were sleeping. This makes little sense. This was an entire guard of highly trained Roman soldiers, and falling asleep on duty was punishable by death.

Further, each of the disciples (individually and separately from each other) were tortured and martyred for proclaiming that Jesus was alive, risen from the dead. Men and women will die for what they believe to be true, though it may actually be false. They do not, however, die for what they know is a lie. If ever a man tells the truth, it is on his deathbed.

Maybe the authorities moved the body? Yet they crucified Jesus to stop people from believing in Him. This also is a weak possibility. If they had Christ's body, they could have paraded it through the streets of Jerusalem. In one fell swoop they would have successfully smothered Christianity in its cradle. That they did not do this bears eloquent testimony to the fact that they did not have the body.

Another theory is that the women, distraught and overcome by grief, missed their way in the dimness of the morning and went to the wrong tomb. In their distress they imagined Christ had risen because the tomb was empty. But again, if the women went to the wrong tomb, why did the high priests and other enemies of the faith not go to the right tomb and produce the body?

"Men and women will die for what they believe to be true, though it may actually be false. They do not, however, die for what they know is a lie."

One other possibility is what some call "the swoon theory." In this view, Christ did not actually die. He was mistakenly reported to be dead, but had swooned from exhaustion, pain, and loss of blood, and in the coolness of the tomb, He revived. (One would have to overlook the fact that they put a spear in his side to medically confirm his death.)

But let us assume for a moment that Christ was buried alive and swooned. Is it possible to believe that He would have survived three days in a damp tomb without food or water or attention of any kind? Would He have had the strength to extricate Himself from the grave clothes, push the heavy stone away from the mouth of the grave, overcome the Roman guards, and walk miles on feet that had been pierced with spikes? It too makes little sense.

However, it wasn't the empty tomb that convinced Jesus' followers of His deity.

Not just the empty tomb.

That alone did not convince them that Jesus actually rose from the dead, was alive, and was God. What convinced them were the number of times that Jesus showed up, in person, in the flesh, and ate with them, and talked with them. Luke, one of the gospel writers, says of Jesus, "He presented Himself to them and gave many convincing proofs that He was alive. He appeared to them over a period of forty days and spoke about the kingdom of God."[26]

Is Jesus God?

All four of the gospel writers give accounts of Jesus physically showing up after His burial, obviously alive. One time that Jesus joined the disciples, Thomas, was not there. When they told him about it, Thomas simply wouldn't believe it. He flatly stated, "Unless I see the nail marks in His hands and put my finger where the nails were, and put my hand into His side, I will not believe it."

One week later, Jesus came to them again, with Thomas now present. Jesus said to Thomas, "Put your finger here; see My hands. Reach out your hand and put it into My side. Stop doubting and believe." Thomas replied, "My Lord and my God!" Jesus told him "Because you have seen Me, you have believed; blessed are those who have not seen and yet have believed."[27]

Your opportunity

Why did Jesus go through all of that? It was so we could know God now, in this life, by believing in Him. Jesus offers us a far more meaningful life, by being in a relationship with Him. Jesus said, "I came that they might have life, and have it abundantly."[28]

You can begin an intimate relationship with Him right now. You can begin to personally know God in this life on earth, and after death into eternity. Here is God's promise to us:

"For God so loved the world, that He gave his only Son, that whoever believes in Him should not perish but have eternal life."[29] Jesus took our sin on himself, on the cross. He chose to receive punishment for our sin, so that our sin would no longer be a barrier between us and Him. Because He fully paid for your sin, He offers you complete forgiveness and a relationship with Him.

Here is how you can begin that relationship. Jesus said, "Behold, I stand at the door [of your heart] and knock; if anyone hears my voice and opens the door, I will come into him."[30] Right now, you can invite Jesus Christ into your life. The words are not important. What matters is that you respond to Him, in light of what He has done for you, and is now offering you.

You could say to Him something like, "Jesus, I believe in you. Thank you for dying on the cross for my sins. I ask you to forgive me and to come into my life right now. I want to know you and follow you. Thank you for coming into my life and giving me a relationship with you, right now. Thank you."

Adapted from *Know Why You Believe* by Paul E. Little, published by Victor Books, copyright (c) 1988, SP Publications, Inc., Wheaton, IL 60187. Used by permission.

Footnotes: (1) Matthew 7:29 (2) Matthew 16:15-16 (3) John 5:18 (4) John 10:33 (5) Mark 14:61-64 (6) John 8:19; 14:7 (7) 12:45; 14:9 (8) 12:44; 14:1 (9) Mark 9:37 (10) John 15:23 (11) John 5:23 (12) John 10:38 (13) John 8:46 (14) 1 Peter 2:22 (15) Matthew 27:54 (16) John 9:25, 32 (17) Mark 4:41 (18) John 11:48 (19) John 14:6 (20) John 8:12 (21) John 10:28 (22) Mark 9:31 (23) 1 Corinthians 15:14 (24) John 10:18 (25) Matthew 26:52,53 (26) Acts 1:3 (27) John 20:24-29 (28) John 10:10 (29) John 3:16 (30) Revelation 3:20

Used with Permission from EveryStudent

https://www.everystudent.com/features/faith.html

Made in United States
Troutdale, OR
06/02/2024